general editor
H. RAMSDEN

ROMANCERO GITANO

For Joyce

FEDERICO GARCÍA LORCA

ROMANCERO GITANO

EDITED WITH INTRODUCTION AND NOTES
BY
H. RAMSDEN

Emeritus Professor of the University of Manchester

MANCHESTER UNIVERSITY PRESS
Manchester and New York

Copyright © Manchester University Press 1988
Introduction, notes etc © Herbert Ramsden 1988

Published by Manchester University Press
Oxford Road, Manchester M13 9NR, UK
and Room 400, 175 Fifth Avenue, New York, NY 10010, USA
www.manchesteruniversitypress.co.uk

Distributed exclusively in the USA by
Palgrave, 175 Fifth Avenue, New York NY 10010, USA

Distributed exclusively in Canada by
UBC Press, University of British Columbia, 2029 West Mall,
Vancouver, BC, Canada V6T 1Z2

British Library Cataloguing-in-Publication Data
A catalogue record for this book is available from the British Library

Library of Congress Cataloging-in-Publication Data
A catalog record for this book is available from the Library of Congress

ISBN 978 0 7190 7825 5

First published 1988 by Manchester University Press

First digital paperback edition 2008

Printed by Lightning Source

CONTENTS

ROMANCERO GITANO

PREFACE

The present edition is intended principally for students of Spanish and for poetry enthusiasts with knowledge of the language. In the Introduction I offer a fairly comprehensive critical study, with special attention to areas where background information is required that the reader may not possess (for example, on the traditional *romance*, so that one can better appreciate Lorca's own use of the *romance* form) and to aspects of the work that seem important but have been generally neglected (most notably its neo-primitivism). An annotated Select Bibliography is appended both as a guide to further reading and as an indication of the main areas of critical attention. For the text itself I have considered manuscripts, early published versions of individual poems and a wide range of editions, concur with Mario Hernández's view that 'la fidelidad extrema a la primera edición obedece a un fetichismo injustificado' (*4*, 201) and finally find myself closest to the revised edition of 1935 published by Espasa-Calpe. In the Endnotes I offer brief practical guidance to the first-time reader but, for fuller commentary, am obliged to refer readers to my companion volume, *Lorca's 'Romancero gitano'. Eighteen Commentaries* (Manchester University Press). For a number of reasons — partly lack of space, but principally the nature of the text and its difficulties and the assumed linguistic competence of the intended reader — the usual end-of-text vocabulary has here been replaced by fuller treatment of vocabulary and syntax within the Endnotes.

1988 H. R.

INTRODUCTION

A DOUBLE BREAK WITH THE PAST

1927 stands out in Spanish literature as the tercentenary year of the death of Luis de Góngora. Poets and critics of the new generation vied with one another in homage to a poet whose greatest work, it was felt, had hitherto been misunderstood and unjustly neglected. Lorca, currently writing *Romancero gitano*, contributed to the homage, initially with a lecture on Góngora's imagery (III, 223–47). What lay behind the Cordoban poet's 'revolución lírica'? he wondered. Góngora was well versed in Latin language and literature and he reacted with distaste to the *defectos*, *imperfecciones* and *sentimientos vulgares* of contemporary Castilian poetry — and to Castile and Castilians in general. 'Todo el polvo de Castilla le llenaba el alma y la sotana de racionero. Sentía que los poemas de los otros eran imperfectos, descuidados, como hechos al desgaire' (III, 228). His aim was a new beauty of language, 'un nuevo método para cazar y plasmar las metáforas', a new means of eternalising the poem by the quality and interaction of its images:

> Y cansado de castellanos y de 'color local', leía su Virgilio con una fruición de hombre sediento de elegancia. Su sensibilidad le puso un microscopio en las pupilas. Vio el idioma castellano lleno de cojeras y de claros, y con su instinto estético fragante empezó a construir una nueva torre de gemas y piedras inventadas que irritó el orgullo de los castellanos en sus palacios de adobes. Se dio cuenta de la fugacidad del sentimiento humano y de lo débiles que son las expresiones espontáneas que solo conmueven en algunos momentos, y quiso que la belleza de su obra radicara en la metáfora limpia de realidades que mueren, metáfora construida con espíritu escultórico y situada en un ambiente extraatmosférico (III, 228–9).

Underlying Góngora's poetic revolution, then, Lorca found two driving forces: the reaction of a cultivated Andalusian against Castile and against established Castilian literature, and the quest for a new and more lasting beauty of language, with emphasis on images and thence also on the senses ('los cinco sentidos corporales', III, 229) rather than on fleeting emotive states. The duality reflects Lorca's own development away from the literature of the generation immediately preceding his own: on the one hand, his reaction against the Castilianism of the so-called 1898 Generation with an affirmation of Andalusian values; on the other, his quest for hard, sense-based imagery in place of the emotive, Romantic-type communication that still persisted, albeit in muted form, in Modernists and writers of 98.

'¡¡Basta ya de Castilla!!'

In 1921 or 1922 Lorca wrote to Fernández Almagro of his plans for the coming summer: 'Este verano, si Dios me ayuda con sus palomitas, haré una obra popular y andalucísima. Voy a viajar un poco por estos pueblos maravillosos, cuyos castillos, cuyas personas parece que nunca han existido para los poetas y ... ¡¡Basta ya de Castilla!!' (III, 717).[1] His tacit allusion to the writers of the 1898 Generation, then in their forties or fifties, seems clear. They too were notable *excursionistas* but their proclaimed quest was for the soul of Spain and the key to this, they believed, lay in Castile: 'lo castellano es, en fin de cuenta, lo castizo' (Unamuno, *OC* I, Madrid 1966, 805); 'Hacíamos excursiones en el tiempo y en el espacio. Visitábamos las vetustas ciudades *castellanas*. Descubríamos y corroborábamos en esas ciudades la continuidad *nacional*' (Azorín, *OC* VI, Madrid 1962, 229; my italics). Inevitably, other regional identities were played down:

> En el aspecto íntimo del arte, para el que busca sensaciones profundas, para el que tiene el espíritu preparado a recibir la más honda revelación de la historia eterna, os digo que lo mejor de España es Castilla, y en Castilla pocas ciudades, si es que hay alguna, superior a Avila. Váyase a Sevilla, váyase a Valencia el que quiera divertirse o distraerse el ánimo, el que quiera matar

---

[1] The letter is undated. The first editor, Antonio Gallego Morell, proposed 'primavera 1923' but Mario Hernández has argued convincingly for the spring of 1921 (*4*, 165) and his dating is accepted by Christopher Maurer (FGL, *Epistolario*, I, Madrid 1983, 32–3) and Christian de Paepe (FGL, *Poema del cante jondo*, Madrid 1986, p. 8). Aguilar 1986 changes from 'primavera 1923' to 1 July 1922 in the belief that the celebration dinner referred to in Lorca's letter (III, 717) was the same as one known to have been held on that date (III, 1241).

unos días viviendo con la sobrehaz del alma; pero el que quiera columbrar lo que pudo antaño haber sido, vivir con el fondo del alma, ése que vaya a Avila; que venga también a Salamanca (1909; Unamuno, I, 275).

It was this sort of thing that Lorca was reacting against in his letter to Fernández Almagro: over-emphasis on Castile and the associated dismissive attitude to Andalusia. But one can have little doubt that he was reacting also against the intellectualism of the writers of 1898: their determinism, their historicism, their emphasis on collective psychology and, inseparable from all this, their concern with national destiny. 'A mí no me hablen de hispanoamericanismo', he said years later in a notably un-1898 declaration; 'Yo no entiendo nada de eso, y me importa absolutamente nada de las carabelas, el descubrimiento, la nación madre y las naciones hijas, y toda la retórica de cartón de los banquetes. Esas son cosas muy serias para señores muy serios y . . . muy aburridos, ¿no le parece a usted?'[2]

In reaction against the characteristic 1898 emphasis on Castile — including examples in his own teenage *Impresiones y paisajes* (1918) — Lorca, in 1921, gave himself up to a campaign of self-immersion in Andalusian culture that was also a campaign of self-discovery. 'Yo vivo de prestado,' he wrote to Sainz de la Maza, 'lo que tengo dentro no es mío, veremos a ver si nazco. Mi alma está absolutamente sin abrir' (III, 782–3), and in the next letter, as though declaring his solution, 'Este año no he vuelto a Madrid porque he estado haciendo *cosas* que no podía realizar en la Villa del Oso por su entraña andaluza y por su ritmo especial [. . .]. Granada me ha dado visiones nuevas y ha llenado mi corazón (demasiado tierno) de cosas imprevistas' (III, 783). He learnt to play the guitar, with daily instruction from two gypsies whose own playing reached 'lo más hondo del sentimiento popular' (III, 776); he enthused over flamenco music, 'una de las creaciones más gigantescas del pueblo español' (III, 776); he wrote the greater part of a book of poems inspired in Andalusian *cante*, *Poema del cante jondo*, 'la primera cosa de *otra orientación mía*' (III, 778); he discovered as much as he could about disappearing traditional puppet plays (III, 776), wrote puppet pieces of his own with musical collaboration from Manuel de Falla (III, 779–80) and planned further puppet plays 'llenos

[2] Cit. Alfredo de la Guardia, *GL* [1941], 4th ed., Buenos Aires 1961, p. 94.

de emoción andaluza y exquisito sentimiento popular' (III, 791). By
the end of 1921 he was also involved in preparations for the forth-
coming *cante jondo* festival, the first ever, organised by the Centro
Artístico of Granada 'con el objeto de estimular en el pueblo el cultivo
de los antiguos cantos, en muchas partes casi absolutamente olvidados'
(official prospectus). Opposition to the festival was strong. *Cante jondo*,
it was claimed, was the song of drunkards, gypsies and good-for-
nothings. By organising a festival, wrote Francisco de Paula Valladar,
Granada was in danger of making itself the laughing-stock of Spain.
Manuel de Falla, 'alma de este Concurso' (III, 196), offered behind-
the-scenes encouragement, advice and scholarly backing to Lorca and
his friends, and in the run-up to the competition Lorca gave his cel-
ebrated lecture on *cante* (III, 195–216).[3] 'No es posible', he argued,
'que las canciones más emocionantes y profundas de nuestra misteriosa
alma estén tachadas de tabernarias y sucias; no es posible que el hilo
que nos une con el Oriente impenetrable quieran amarrarlo en el mástil
de la guitarra juerguista' (III, 195–6). Against the Castilianism of the
98 Generation Lorca here proclaims proudly the soul and culture of
Andalusia and its oriental heritage. Not surprisingly, the most cel-
ebrated writers of 98 were not among the twenty-eight artists and intellec-
tuals who responded to requests for support for the Centro Artístico's
initiative. Andalusia played a leading role in nineteenth-century Spain,
wrote Ortega y Gasset a few years later in a famous essay, and it may
become influential again. But it is unlikely that we shall again be
moved by *cante jondo* or smugglers. 'Toda esta quincalla meridional nos
enoja y fastidia.'[4] It is a typically 98 attitude and it contrasts notably with
Lorca's. Apart from his enthusiasm for *cante*, 'una de las creaciones
artísticas populares más fuertes del mundo' (III, 215), he informed
Jorge Guillén in 1926 of his plan to write a poem on the Andalusian
bandit Diego Corrientes (III, 896) and the following year proposed a
book of *crímenes* to José María de Cossío (III, 938). The difference

---

[3] Falla's important pamphlet, *El 'cante jondo' (Canto primitivo andaluz)*,
seems to have circulated freely in manuscript among supporters of the
festival, for its arguments were much used in articles, submissions and press
reports before it finally appeared, anonymously, in published form
(Granada: Urania, 1922). The first half of Lorca's lecture (III, 195–204) is
based closely on Falla's study.
[4] 'Teoría de Andalucía' (*El Sol*, April 1927), collected in *Teoría de
Andalucía y otros ensayos*, Madrid 1944, pp. 11–35 (quotation, p. 17).

from Ortega and the writers of 98 is clear. As Lorca's repeated refer-
ences to *sentimiento popular* and *arte popular* show, the cult of the
pueblo desconocido continues. But from 1921 at least his emphasis is
wholly different: the notion of national destiny is absent, the quest for
significance (Unamuno's *honda revelación de la historia eterna*) has
yielded to a more immediate response to people and culture for their
own sake, lamentation for the past and admonitions about the future to
a more naked delight in the present, psychological probing and intel-
lectualising historicism to sensation and instantaneity of experience
and expression. But the shift of emphasis from Castile to Andalusia
was not merely, as the earlier quotation from Unamuno might suggest,
a shift from the *fondo del alma* to the *sobrehaz del alma*. In immersing
himself in Andalusian popular culture Lorca made contact also with
neglected primitive forces and art forms that had no place in the esta-
blished cultural hierarchy. His defiant *andalucismo* marks the appear-
ance of a new generation in Spanish literature.

Pruning the Lyrical Tree

In his lecture on *cante jondo* Lorca emphasised the special relevance
and appeal of *cante* to the modern poet:

> Una de las maravillas del cante jondo, aparte de la esencial
> melódica, consiste en los poemas.
> Todos los poetas que actualmente nos ocupamos, en más o
> menos escala, en la poda y cuidado del demasiado frondoso árbol
> lírico que nos dejaron los románticos y los postrománticos, que-
> damos asombrados ante dichos versos.
> Las más infinitas gradaciones del Dolor y la Pena, puestas al
> servicio de la expresión más pura y exacta, laten en los tercetos y
> cuartetos de la siguiriya y sus derivados.
> No hay nada, absolutamente nada, igual en toda España, ni en
> estilización, ni en ambiente, ni en justeza emocional (III, 205).

In the traditional lines 'Cerco tiene la luna, / mi amor ha muerto', he
continued, 'hay mucho más misterio que en todos los dramas de
Maeterlinck' (III, 205), and later, 'Es admirable cómo a través de las
construcciones líricas un sentimiento va tomando forma y cómo llega a
concrecionarse en una cosa casi material' (III, 209). For Lorca, it
seems, the anonymous poetry of *cante jondo* is characterised especially
by the interplay of specific reference and uncontoured resonances. At
times, as in 'Cerco tiene la luna ...', it is a real-life element that is

notably specific; at other times, as in the following *siguiriya*, 'gitana y andalucísima' (III, 211), it is the imagery:

> Si mi corazón tuviera
> birieritas e cristar [vidrieritas de cristal],
> te asomaras y lo vieras
> gotas de sangre llorar.

In each case the specific reference sets up wider resonances.

Cante jondo, then, is relevant to both aspects of Lorca's double break with the past: on the one hand, since it is profoundly Andalusian, it serves as a nucleus of opposition to the excessive Castilianism of the 1898 Generation; on the other hand, by its *expresión pura y exacta*, it suggests a means of escape from the over-profuse lyricism of Romantic tradition. Lorca finds a similar duality in Góngora: on the one hand, he is profoundly Andalusian in his use of imagery; on the other, with his imagery he is 'padre de la lírica moderna' (III, 227). The following much quoted lines merit special attention:

> El lenguaje está hecho a base de imágenes, y nuestro pueblo tiene una riqueza magnífica de ellas. Llamar alero a la parte saliente del tejado es una imagen magnífica; o llamar a un dulce tocino de cielo o suspiros de monja, [son] otras muy graciosas, por cierto, y muy agudas; llamar a una cúpula media naranja es otra; y así, infinidad. En Andalucía la imagen popular llega a extremos de finura y sensibilidad maravillosas, y las transformaciones son completamente gongorinas.
>
> A un cauce profundo que discurre lento por el campo lo llaman un *buey de agua*, para indicar su volumen, su acometividad y su fuerza; y yo he oído decir a un labrador de Granada: 'A los mimbres les gusta estar siempre en la *lengua* del río.' Buey de agua y lengua de río son dos imágenes hechas por el pueblo y que responden a una manera de ver ya muy de cerca de don Luis de Góngora (III, 224).

Anyone who has lived in an Andalusian environment and observed Andalusian linguistic usage will agree: the *andaluz*, in everyday speech, is notable for his use of imagery. Thus, a friend who has recently undergone a by-pass operation under local anaesthetic tells, with complete naturalness, how he was able to watch the surgeon insert the *macarrón* (*macaroni*, an image of the arterial graft); another, as he washes his car, notices that he has left *llorones* (*weepings*, an image of runs or streaks) on the windscreen; yet another calls his wife because his grandchild has fallen *y se ha hecho una graná* (*granada, pomegranate*, an image of a contused wound). It is something that one associates immediately with Andalusian speech and the last example is echoed in *Romancero gitano*:

> Juan Antonio el de Montilla
> rueda muerto la pendiente,
> su cuerpo lleno de lirios
> y una granada en las sienes (3:17–20).

To the Castilian, who does not use the expression, the image causes problems; to the Andalusian, I find, it does not. But the image of *granada* as a contused wound is here accompanied by another image that I have not heard used in popular speech: that of *lirios* (*irises*) as stab-wounds, here of knives, elsewhere of a bull's horn (I, 552). As an arch-Andalusian, Lorca not only incorporates established imagery; with his remarkable power of visualisation and association he also creates corresponding images of his own.

We can best see this by examining a passage from one of his most exuberantly Andalusian letters and considering its relevance to the style of *Romancero gitano*:

> ¡Si vieras cómo está Andalucía! Para andar hay que hacer galerías en la luz de oro como los topos en su medio oscuro. Las sedas brillantes miguel-angelizan los culos de las mujeres opulentas. Los gallos clavan banderillas de lujo en el testuz del amanecer y yo me pongo moreno de sol y de luna llena ... (1925; III, 920).

After an initial exclamation that characteristically emphasises visual perception (cf. 'Todas las imágenes se abren en el campo visual', III, 230) he starts by emphasising the light: golden light (metaphor) that is so dense that one has to tunnel one's way through it (metaphor) like moles through their own dark realm (simile). In the next sentence he creates a metaphorical neologism, *miguel-angelizan* (since Michelangelo's paintings, like his sculptures, are notable for their sculpted fullness of form), to bring out, as the shimmering silks bring out, the repleteness of hidden contours. Then, with the personification of cocks as *banderilleros* and the personification — or animalisation — of the morning as a bull, the cockcrows (sound) are presented synaesthetically — and metaphorically — as a piercing (sight) of the bull's neck. Finally, in an effective example of zeugma, *me pongo moreno* is applied to juxtaposed differences of register: that of the sun, literal and physical, and that of the moon, magical and emotive. In all four cases one notes characteristic features. Firstly, of course, the writer's strikingly Andalusian sensitivity to sense perceptions: 'Un poeta', said Lorca in his Góngora lecture, 'tiene que ser profesor en los cinco sentidos corporales' (III, 229). Secondly, the manner in which, with a mental and imaginative agility that one again associates with Andalusians, he superimposes different sense perceptions or finds in a particular sense perception a springboard to something far wider. 'Para poder ser dueño de las más bellas imágenes', Lorca continued in his lecture, '[el poeta] tiene que abrir puertas de comunicación en todos ellos [los sentidos] y con mucha frecuencia ha de superponer sus sensaciones y aun de disfrazar sus naturalezas' (III, 229); 'La metáfora une dos mundos antagónicos por medio de un salto ecuestre que da la imaginación' (III, 230). Finally — and here I hesitate to claim this as a particularly Andalusian characteristic — one notes that all the images are functional rather than purely decorative, with expressive emphasis on the density of light, on the women's Michelangelised bottoms, on the fiesta-like exhilaration of the new day and on the magic and mystery that underlie the initially prosaic *me pongo moreno*.

Similar images appear throughout *Romancero gitano*. The first, for example, recalls lines from the 'Romance de la Guardia Civil española':

> ¡Oh ciudad de los gitanos!
> La Guardia Civil se aleja
> por un túnel de silencio
> mientras las llamas te cercan (15:117–20).

The *túnel de silencio* is comparable to the *galerías de luz* and the moles' tunnelling through their own dark realm, with similar emphasis on density: in this case, the density of darkness, silence, fear and destruction that the Civil Guard has created with its passing. The next image recalls lines from 'San Miguel (Granada)':

> Vienen manolas comiendo
> semillas de girasoles,
> los culos grandes y ocultos
> como planetas de cobre (8:33–6).

Far from the illusioned *girasoles* with which the poem opened, the coarsely strident *manola* girls from the popular quarter of Granada are shown chewing the traditional *pepitas*, with bottoms big and hidden — but only just, since we are invited to consider contour, firmness and colour as well as size — like planets of copper. By simile Lorca here suggests the same copious forms as in the metaphorically Michelangelised backsides evoked in his letter. In his third image Lorca presented cocks as *banderilleros* piercing with their cries the neck of the bull-like dawn. The image in the opening lines of 'Romance de la pena negra' is not wholly dissimilar:

> Las piquetas de los gallos
> cavan buscando la aurora,
> cuando por el monte oscuro
> baja Soledad Montoya (7:1–4).

Picks have replaced *banderillas*, and the dawn, since it has not yet appeared, is not personified. But there is comparable metaphor in the image of picks' digging and similar synaesthesia in the visual rendering of sound. Finally, as a parallel to Lorca's zeugmatic *moreno de sol y de luna llena* I quote two lines from 'Romance de la pena negra', both relevant to Soledad Montoya: *huele a caballo y a sombra* (7:6) and *agrio de espera y de boca* (7:26). In each case a common indication of sense perception (*huele a* and *agrio de*) is accompanied by a physical element (*caballo, boca*) and by a less clearly contoured abstract and emotive element (*sombra, espera*). As in his letter, Lorca is here opening 'puertas de comunicación' and not only between the senses. As elsewhere in *Romancero gitano*, 'por medio de un salto ecuestre que da la imaginación', the physical here-and-now becomes a springboard to mysterious forces and denied illusion.

In the above, guided by Lorca himself, I have pointed to two aspects of the poet's indebtedness to Andalusia: *cante jondo* in which he found specific references allied to wider resonances of mystery and lamentation, and popular linguistic usage in which he noted, as in Góngora, striking visual sensitivity and imaginative creativity resulting in *extremos de finura y sensibilidad maravillosas*. As we shall see, Lorca's indebtedness to Andalusian culture is far greater than this, but from a purely stylistic point of view we have identified the two most notable features of his style in *Romancero gitano* and in the above comments it has become difficult to maintain the separation. As my comments on the Civil Guard's *túnel de silencio* and the zeugmatic 'springboard to mysterious forces and denied illusion' show, Lorca's typically Andalusian images and transpositions serve also to set up *cante*-like resonances of mystery and lamentation. Under the influence of his *andalucismo*, it seems, Lorca has not only broken with the Castilianism of the 1898 Generation; he has also found a way out of the explicit emotionalism of Romantic tradition. In place of abstracted emotion he proposes — and offers — sense-based imagery; in place of explicitness he finds — and will exploit — mysterious, uncontoured resonances. This duality will be with us throughout the following pages.

But we should do Lorca an injustice if we were to circumscribe the significance of his poetic revolution to mere *andalucismo*. What he finds in Andalusian linguistic usage is a new freshness and directness of vision. It is something that one associates, for example, with the un-inhibited creativity of young children: 'An aeroplane that cracks the sky', 'Stars that prick the sky', 'Trees that prick the child Jesus' (since Jesus is in Heaven), 'Daddy, I'm raining' (= crying) ....[5] It is something that one associates, too, with the whole imagist movement in literature during the second and third decades of the twentieth century. The subject has still to be explored for its relevance to Lorca and this is not the place. A few brief indications, however, are indispensable. As a basis for illustration I find no better way than to refer to three essays that in many ways served as manifestos of the age: Ezra Pound's 'A Retrospect' (1911–17; collected 1918), T. E. Hulme's 'Romanticism and Classicism' (1913–14; published 1924) and T. S. Eliot's 'Tradition and the Individual Talent' (1919). All proclaimed a reaction against the emotionalism of the Romantics ('emotional slither', Pound; 'the eternal gases', Hulme; 'Poetry is not a turning loose of emotion', Eliot) and all emphasised the need for harder, more precise imagery ('harder and saner [...], as much like granite as it can be', Pound; 'dry hardness', images as 'the very essence of an intuitive language', Hulme; not 'emotion recollected in tranquillity' but 'concentration and a new thing resulting from the concentration', Eliot). As for the mysterious reson-ances referred to by Lorca, these were basic to the earlier and continu-ing Symbolist tradition: refined Romanticism, 'poetry stripped of its perdamnable rhetoric' (Pound). W. B. Yeats, who according to Pound did the stripping, was the principal Symbolist poet in English and in the following lines he exemplifies his poetic ideal:

[5] All are specific examples from my own children's store; compare respectively Lorca's 'cielos hechos añicos' (I, 517), 'las estrellas clavan / rejones al agua gris' (I, 419), '¡Arboles! / ¿Habéis sido flechas / caídas del azul?' (I, 113) and the earlier mentioned Andalusian use of *llorones* to indicate streaks.

There are no lines with more melancholy beauty than these by Burns:
The white moon is setting behind the white wave.
And Time is setting with me, O!
and these lines are perfectly symbolical [...]. If one begins the reverie [on symbolical writing] with any beautiful lines that one can remember, one finds they are like those by Burns ('The Symbolism of Poetry', 1900).

Example and comment are both strikingly akin to Lorca's own, referred to earlier:

Hay coplas en que el temblor lírico llega a un punto donde no pueden llegar sino contadísimos poetas:
Cerco tiene la luna,
mi amor ha muerto.
En estos dos versos populares hay mucho más misterio que en todos los dramas de Maeterlinck (III, 205).

In Andalusian culture, it seems, Lorca found a key to the poetic ideals of the twentieth century. It merits explanation. In the present context a tentative paragraph must suffice.

Lorca's first book of poetry, *Libro de poemas*, was published in 1921. It contains poems written in 1918–20 and throws much light on the poet's evolving style. In particular one sees that his poetry became notably more avant-garde after his move from provincial Granada to the Residencia de Estudiantes in Madrid (spring 1919). But by the end of 1920, after eighteen months of contact with avant-garde theory and practice, Lorca was apparently coming to realise that much of what he most valued in modern poetry was to be found, potentially at least, in Andalusian culture. Every nation and every race, says Eliot in the above quoted essay, has its own creative turn of mind. Similarly, it seems, with every race there are moments when its creative turn of mind is especially attuned to the creative ideals of the age. So it was with Andalusia in the 1920s. It matters little that Ezra Pound, an American, had already shown the way or that Ramón Gómez de la Serna, a native of Madrid, preceded Lorca with similar imagery. It was in Andalusia especially that Lorca felt able to live and breathe his new poetics. And not only Lorca. There were few Andalusians in the intellectualising and emotive 1898 Generation; in reality only the Castilianised and not very intellectualising Antonio Machado. In Lorca's own generation, on the other hand, half the most notable poets were Andalusian and they are among the great poets both of the European avant-garde and of Spanish literature: Lorca himself, Vicente Aleixandre, Rafael Alberti and Luis Cernuda. With Juan Ramón Jiménez, another Andalusian, as their early poetic mentor, and Góngora, yet another Andalusian, as their great poet from the past, it seems difficult not to accept a significant relationship between *andalucismo* and avant-garde literature. In *Romancero gitano*, certainly, it is difficult to separate the two.

ROMANCERO GITANO: THE IMMEDIATE APPEAL

Romancero gitano is one of the most immediately appealing books of poetry in Spanish literature. It is also one of the most difficult. To understand this one can think of a stone thrown into a pond. From a specific point of impact successive circles radiate. So it is with Lorca's poetry: on the one hand it is intensely present, specific and physical; on the other hand it sets up resonances that carry us away from the mere here-and-now to something far wider. In his lecture on Góngora's poetic imagery Lorca noted a similar duality: 'forma y radio de acción', 'núcleo central y una redonda perspectiva en torno de él' (III, 230). Basically, the immediate appeal of Lorca's poetry lies in its vivid here-and-nowness: specific point of impact, 'forma', 'núcleo central'; its greatness — and much of its difficulty — in the interaction of this here-and-nowness with wider resonances: successive circles of significance, 'radio de acción', 'redonda perspectiva'. The equation is not absolute. Some of the difficulties lie in aspects of the work's here-and-nowness and some of its immediate appeal is attributable to easily accessible radiations of mystery, magic and wider significance. But the distinction is generally valid and it will serve as a basis for exposition. In the present section I shall emphasise *lo inmediato*, the immediate presence of Lorca's world in *Romancero gitano*; in succeeding sections I shall consider the more difficult question of wider and less contoured resonances.

Characters, Conflicts, Settings, Props

As the title *Romancero gitano* suggests, we are concerned with the gypsy and his world. Setting and protagonists could scarcely be better suited to the poet's emphasis on present experience. 'El andaluz', said Ortega, 'tiene un sentido vegetal de la existencia y vive con preferencia en su piel' (*Teoría de Andalucía* ..., 32). And as the Andalusian is noted in other parts of Spain for his ability to extract maximum enjoyment from the passing present and for his lack of concern with hypothetical problems of the future, so the gypsy is noted for these same qualities among Andalusians. In many ways he is the arch-*andaluz*. Even when allowance is made for Lorca's idealising vision, there is a considerable basis of truth in his following comment: 'El libro en conjunto, aunque se llama gitano, es el poema de Andalucía; y lo llamo gitano porque el gitano es lo más elevado, lo más profundo, más aristocrático de mi país, lo más representativo de su modo y el que guarda el ascua, la sangre y el alfabeto de la verdad andaluza y universal' (III, 340). One notes, for example, Antoñito's easy-going progress to Seville to see the bullfight, a switch in his hand and his glossy black locks over his forehead, carelessly throwing lemons into the irrigation channels for the sheer joy of seeing the water turn to gold (11:1–12). And his child-like vanity about his dandified appearance:

> Zapatos color corinto,
> medallones de marfil,
> y este cutis amasado
> con aceituna y jazmín (12:29–32).

And Saint Gabriel's refined elegance (10:1–14) and his delightfully Andalusian — and even Sevillian — announcement of glad tidings to the gypsy girl Anunciación:

> —Dios te salve, Anunciación.
> Morena de maravilla.
> Tendrás un niño más bello
> que los tallos de la brisa (10:43–6).

And the gypsy nun, embroidering humble gillyflowers on an altar-cloth and dreaming of the more colourful *flores de su fantasía* that she would like to embroider:

> ¡Qué girasol! ¡Qué magnolia
> de lentejuelas y cintas!
> ¡Qué azafranes y qué lunas,
> en el mantel de la misa! (5:13–16).

There is a gypsy Don Juan, too, who recounts a sexual adventure with a married woman and, having revealed the most piquant details of his experience, alleges discretion and declines to reveal what the girl *said* to him (6:40–1). Here as so often in *Romancero gitano* it is less Lorca the lyric poet who strikes us than Lorca the dramatist. One finds something similar in Soledad Montoya's pert response to the narrator when he asks about her early morning sally:

> —Soledad: ¿por quién preguntas
> sin compaña y a estas horas?
> —Pregunte por quien pregunte,
> dime: ¿a ti qué se te importa?
> Vengo a buscar lo que busco,
> mi alegría y mi persona (7:9–14).

Even suffering, it seems, cannot suppress the gypsy sense of pride. They are characters, as one might say in Spanish, *de una pieza*: whole, erect, authentic, uncomplicated, fully themselves and fully alive — even in their acceptance of death: like Juan Antonio of Montilla, pierced by knives, who rides off on a cross of fire along the highway to death (3:17–22); like Amargo too, all torment past, finding his proud profile again in death (*fijaba sobre el muro / su soledad con descanso*), with a shroud whose straight lines epitomise the statuesque dignity of his passing (14:52–7). 'España', said Lorca, 'es el país de los perfiles [. . .]. Todo se dibuja y limita de la manera más exacta. Un muerto es más muerto en España que en cualquiera otra parte del mundo' (III, 285). He was referring to Spanish nursery rhymes, but the observation is relevant also to *Romancero gitano* with its emphasis on physical and psychological clarity of outline. Complexity and subtlety of characterisation is not his aim. Hamlet's oscillations and self-probing would be wholly out of place in the elemental world of *Romancero gitano*. Lorca's gypsies act *porque sí*, with an uninhibited, almost childlike response to life, impelled by forces and passions that they themselves do not understand and that we as readers are not invited to probe. Innocence and naiveté, childlike vanity and exuberance and joy in life, elegance and pride and swagger, indignation and explosiveness, uninhibited weeping and lamentation — all mingle in characters who are often physically appealing and never physically repellent. 'Por un morenico de color verde,' wrote Cervantes — in lines that recall Lorca's own gypsy, *moreno de verde luna* (11:5)—, '¿cuál es la fogosa que no se pierde?'[1] The attractiveness of Lorca's gypsies is an important aspect of the work's immediate appeal.

---

[1] *Rinconete y Cortadillo*, in Cervantes, *OC*, Madrid: Aguilar, 1962, p. 848.

Lorca's gypsies, in joy as in suffering, are fully alive. But they are also under threat, and this further involves our sympathies. The Civil Guard, for example, the traditional antagonists of the gypsies, appear in several poems. And because they are the traditional antagonists, in real life as in literature, the conflict takes on wider resonances and strikes familiar chords. Besides, whatever realists may say about life's being neither white nor black but universal grey, with good and evil mingling on all sides, the popular imagination looks for heroes and villains and Lorca, as the ostensible gypsy narrator, responds. Whereas his gypsies are commonly presented as individuals (*Juan Antonio el de Montilla*; *Antonio Torres Heredia*) and are enhanced in a host of ways (cf. below: 'Character enhancement'), the civil guards are referred to only collectively (*guardia civil caminera*; *guardias civiles borrachos*) or metonymically (*cinco tricornios*; *capas siniestras*). In the former case the effect is to depersonalise them; in the latter case it serves also to debase them by association. Moreover, *tricornios*, besides referring specifically to civil guards, recalls a long tradition of abused power (cf. Alarcón's *El sombrero de tres picos*), and the *capas siniestras*, with their *manchas de tinta y de cera* (15:4), remind us that the Civil Guard is representative of a wider oppression, suggestive of both state bureaucracy (*tinta*) and church obscurantism (*cera*). The conflict between gypsies and civil guards, then, has resonances that Spanish readers at least recognise immediately, and Barea was doubtless correct, especially in the aftermath of the Spanish Civil War, to emphasise this as a further aspect of Lorca's popular appeal.

But one misrepresents the range and character of *Romancero gitano* if one concentrates too exclusively on the conflict between gypsies and Civil Guard. Civil guards appear in five of the eighteen poems (3, 4, 11, 12, 15) and even if carabineers (2), Roman centurions (16) and Old Testament *negros* (18) also are included — since they too represent law and order — the number rises to only eight. Besides, Poem 15, on which Barea and other politically inspired critics principally base their case, is the only *romance* where the civil guards are clear and blatant oppressors (though there is an element of oppression also in Poems 4 and 11) and in Poem 12 they are even called upon for help by a dying gypsy (12:37–8). In fact, as the most superficial survey shows, the Civil Guard is but one of many elements of oppression for Lorca's gypsies. In 'Romance de la luna, luna' it is the mythical moon that comes down and steals a child away; in 'Preciosa y el aire', the big-man wind that accosts a gypsy girl and pursues her in sexual fury; in 'Reyerta', fellow gypsies, influenced perhaps by black angels; in 'Romance sonámbulo', life's whole denial of longed-for illusion; in 'La monja gitana', the torment of convent life for a gypsy girl .... On all sides, it seems, the gypsy's longed-for enjoyment of life is hedged about with restraints imposed by fellow men, by society, by institutions, by telluric and cosmic forces, by fate and life and death. It is the basic conflict of vitality and repression that one finds throughout Lorca's writings, and the outcome of gypsy awareness of this, in *Romancero gitano*, is the *pena negra* of Andalusian tradition. It finds its clearest expression in Soledad Montoya and the 'Romance de la pena negra', but as Lorca himself pointed out, *pena* is present throughout the book (III, 340). Beyond gypsy characters and gypsy actions the poet finds ultimately, as in his other writings, the mystery and anguish of man's denied striving and illusions. It is a theme to which the reader can easily respond, especially in a world of increasing regimentation and depersonalisation.

Lorca's gypsies are notable for their vivid, physical presence and I know of no book of poetry where there is so much specific reference to the human body: *cuerpo, cabeza, pelo, barba, ojos, nariz, boca, lengua, garganta, torso, espalda* and at least a dozen more. Actions are presented with similar immediacy. In Lorca's own words — about poetry that he much admired —, 'Todo se dibuja y limita de la manera más exacta' (III, 285). One can say something similar of his settings, with place names (Guadalquivir, Seville, Montilla, Jerez de la Frontera . . .) and typical scenic elements (*limones, higuera, olivares, pitas* . . .) that immediately suggest Andalusia and, together with a host of other references, serve to localise also the more generic indications of landscape (*monte, sierra, barranco* . . .), skyscape (*luna, estrellas, nubes* . . .) and — less frequently — seascape (*el barco sobre la mar, el mar baila por la playa, ribera del mar*). But we are far from realism. Antoñito has typical gypsy black locks and olive complexion rather than realistically exclusive warts or harelip, and Jerez de la Frontera has towers and flags rather than a specifically identifiable — and therefore exclusive — tower or flag. With individual gypsies and their actions as with settings Lorca can thus pass easily from specific reference to wider resonances,[2] and nature helps in the transition, not merely as a setting but as an

---

[2] The nearest apparent exception to the above is in the foretold *lunar y tres heridas* (10:54). But the wider resonances there lie precisely in those characteristics, and the *tres heridas* are significantly carried over to the protagonist of the following two poems (*Tres golpes de sangre*, 12:41).

active participant. Thus, instead of a merely realistic background *monte* one finds a *monte oscuro* whose darkness complements the dark torment of character and action (7:3), and an *aire de poniente* appropriately accompanies Juan of Montilla's death (3:36) and *cielos quemados* are at one with Olalla's burnt body (16:68) and *nubes paradas* suggest shock and horror at Amnón's rape of his sister (18:84) and olives turn pale at the wind's pursuit of Preciosa (2:34) or await Antoñito's fateful night of Capricorn (11:21–2) .... I recall again Lorca's enthusiasm for the following traditional lines:

> Cerco tiene la luna,
> mi amor ha muerto.

The sight of an impressive Andalusian lunar halo is awe-inspiring in itself. The suggestion that it is related to human destiny fills one with a sense of mystery and apprehension. Lorca creates a similar sense of mystery by suggesting the involvement of nature — and of the cosmos itself — in the fate of his characters. It is a subject to which we shall return. It merits mention here, however, because much of the impact is immediately apparent and, as Lorca's examples from traditional sources demonstrate, one insults the untutored reader by assuming that he is capable of responding only to the physical here-and-now. There are many sophisticated resonances in *Romancero gitano* that he will not easily respond to, but in echoes of mystery and magic and popular tradition one is impressed by how much unlettered Andalusians do capture — at times more than academic commentators — and my present study has gained much from their observations. The main thing, for any reader, is that he should find in each reading sufficient impact and incentive to carry him on to further readings and thus, step by step, to a fuller awareness and appreciation of one of the masterpieces of twentieth-century poetry.

I conclude with a brief reference to what I indicate in my title as props: gypsy trades (anvils, copper articles, rings and necklaces ...) and relevant activities (horsemanship, bullfighting, smuggling, bartering ...), gypsy spells and superstitions, saints and archangels, local fiestas and processions and celebrations. One can point to the appeal of the exotic and to the inherent interest and excitement of the associated action. But it is again difficult to dissociate the here-and-now from its wider resonances. For the moment I refer only to one of Lorca's most notable props, the knife, and recall a quotation from his *Poema del cante jondo* (I, 236):

AMARGO. Un cuchillo no tiene que ser más que un cuchillo.
JINETE. Se equivoca.
AMARGO. Gracias.
JINETE. Los cuchillos de oro se van solos al corazón. Los de plata
cortan el cuello como una brizna de hierba.
AMARGO. ¿No sirven para partir el pan?
JINETE. Los hombres parten el pan con las manos.
AMARGO. ¡Es verdad!
    (*El caballo se inquieta.*)

Amargo's prosaic associations (akin to the 'núcleo central') are contrasted with the Jinete's death associations (with wider 'redonda perspectiva') and the prosaic associations are then cast aside, leaving death as the knife's only function. As for the *caballo [que] se inquieta*, another characteristic prop, one can compare its awareness of threatening misfortune to that of the *caballo malherido / [que] llamaba a todas las puertas* (15:29–30) and the *caballo de larga cola* that heralds the martyrdom of Saint Olalla (16:1–2). As ever in Lorca, the vividly presented here-and-now serves as a pointer to mystery, magic, misfortune ....

The 'Romance' Tradition

All the above — characters, conflicts, settings, elements of gypsy life — are potentially appealing in themselves. But how does the poet make them accessible to his reader? The necessary starting-point is his use of the *romance*, the most traditional and popular of all Spanish verse forms, most commonly octosyllabic, with a stressed seventh syllable and a single assonance on even lines (e.g. Poem 1: *nardos, mirando, brazos* ...). Basically narrative, the *romance* was intended originally not for reading but for public singing or recitation and Lorca, with his delight and skill in recitation and his misgivings about seeing his poems published ('*muertos definitivamente*', III, 902), is commonly likened to a medieval *juglar* (*minstrel*). In the impact of his recitations too, for many of his *romances* were learnt and recited by others long before they appeared in print. In many ways, after the effusive adventure *romances* of the Romantics and the ethereal lyrical *romance* created by Juan Ramón Jiménez, *Romancero gitano* marks a return to a more traditional type of *romance*, short, compact and centred on a single action or event. It is a world of sophisticated primitivism, elemental in its concerns — machismo, bravery, honour, sex, betrayal,

revenge, bloodshed, death ... — but elevated in tone, with no un-
necessary details to detract from essentialised character and action, no
emotive woolliness to diffuse physical contours, no intellectualising
abstractions or explanations and no reflective didacticism. The em-
phasis, in Lorca as in traditional ballad literature, is on immediacy of
impact. The language is correspondingly direct, with basic vocabulary
and uncomplicated syntax.

One can see this initially in his opening lines. Like the traditional
juglar Lorca seeks immediately to seize our attention. Sometimes —
most frequently — he arouses interest by a simple indication of appear-
ance on scene, usually with brief physical placing:

La luna vino a la fragua (1:1)   Cf. De Antequera partió el moro
                                                        (*RVC* 74)

Coches cerrados llegaban   Paseábase el rey moro
a las orillas de juncos (9:1–2)   por la ciudad de Granada
                                                        (*RVC* 85)

Por una vereda   A caza iban, a caza,
venía Don Pedro (17:1–2).   los cazadores del rey.
                                                        (*RVC* 119)[3]

At other times he plunges us directly into action or crisis:

En la mitad del barranco   Cf. Cercada tiene a Baeza
las navajas de Albacete,   ese arráez Andalla Mir,
bellas de sangre contraria,   con ochenta mil peones,
relucen como los peces (3:1–4)   caballeros cinco mil
                                                        (*RVC*-A 18)

¡Mi soledad sin descanso! (14:1)   Doliente estaba, doliente,
                                                   ese buen rey don Fernando.
                                                        (*RVC* 35)

---

[3] *RVC* — *Romances viejos castellanos (Primavera y flor de romances)*, ed.
Wolf and Hofmann [1856], re-edited and supplemented by M. Menéndez
y Pelayo [1899], 2nd ed., Madrid 1928. *RVC*-A — Menéndez y Pelayo's
Apéndice I (in vol. II of the above). The accompanying numbers are poem
numbers. In volume III (1923), however, the poem numbering is complex
and I here use volume and page references, e.g. *RVC* III, 176. In what
follows above I quote also from two other *romance* collections: *RC* —
Romancero del Cid, collected by Juan de Escobar (1614), ed. Ignacio
Bauer, Madrid, 3rd ed., [1925?]; *RGen* — *Romancero general (1600, 1604,
1605)*, ed. Angel González Palencia, 2 vols., Madrid 1947. In both cases I
identify by poem numbering.

Or he allows his protagonist to appear, prologue-like, with a preview of the action:

Y que yo me la llevé al río   Cf. Yo me era mora Moraima,
creyendo que era mozuela,   morilla de un bel catar;
pero tenía marido (6:1–3).   cristiano vino a mi puerta,
                                         cuitada, por me engañar.
                                                        (*RVC* 132)

Also, in opening lines as elsewhere, the present tense serves frequently to bring a past event close to us:

Por la calle brinca y corre   Cf. En Santa Gadea de Burgos
caballo de larga cola,   do juran los hijosdalgo,
mientras juegan o dormitan   allí le toma la jura
viejos soldados de Roma.   el Cid al rey castellano.
          (16:1–4)   (*RVC* 52)

And different verb tenses are often strangely juxtaposed, at times with striking effect:

La luna vino a la fragua   Cf. De Francia salió la niña,
con su polisón de nardos.   de Francia la bien guarnida;
El niño la mira, mira.   perdido lleva el camino,
El niño la está mirando (1:1–4).   perdida lleva la guía.
                                                        (*RVC* 154a)

Among other notable similarities the following are especially relevant to reader and audience involvement and thus to Lorca's immediacy of appeal:

attention-prompting apostrophes to the reader/audience:

¿Pero quién vendrá? ¿Y por   Cf. Hélo, hélo, por dó viene
    dónde?   el moro por la calzada
              (4:21)   (*RVC* 55)

exclamations to highlight aspects of an action, scene or character:

¡Qué girasol! ¡Qué magnolia   Cf. ¡Cuánto del hidalgo moro!
de lentejuelas y cintas!   ¡Cuánta de la yegua baya!
¡Qué azafranes y qué lunas,   ¡Cuánta de la lanza en puño!
en el mantel de la misa! (5:13–16)   ¡Cuánta de la adarga blanca!
                                                        (*RVC* 72)

the frequent interspersing of narrative with dialogue:

—Huye luna, luna, luna,   Cf. —Bien seas venido, el moro,
que ya siento sus caballos.   buena sea tu venida.
—Niño, déjame, no pises   —Alá te mantenga, el rey,
mi blancor almidonado (1:17–20)   con toda tu compañía
                                              (*RVC* 74)

various forms of address by the apparent narrator to one of his characters:[4]

to exhort:

¡Preciosa, corre, Preciosa,   Cf. A las armas, Moriscote,
que te coge el viento verde!   si las has en voluntad:
¡Preciosa, corre, Preciosa!   los franceses son entrados
¡Míralo por dónde viene!   los que en romería van
                    (2:37–40)   (*RVC*-A 29)

to rebuke:

Antonio, ¿quién eres tú?   Cf. ¡Cuán traidor eres,
Si te llamaras Camborio,   Marquillos!
hubieras hecho una fuente   ¡Cuán traidor de corazón!
de sangre con cinco chorros   Por dormir con tu señora
                    (11:29–32)   habías muerto a tu señor
                                              (*RVC* 120)

or to warn:

¡Ay Antoñito el Camborio   Cf. ¡Rey don Sancho, rey don
digno de una Emperatriz!   Sancho,
Acuérdate de la Virgen   no digas que no te aviso,
porque te vas a morir (12: 33–6)   que dentro de Zamora
                                              un alevoso ha salido!
                                                      (*RVC* 45)

---

[4] Usually in traditional *romances* it is not in fact the narrator who speaks but one of the characters. But when the words open the poem and the speaker is identified only later or has been eliminated in oral transmission (cf. elimination in *RVC* 45, 73, vs presence in *RVC* 43, 73a) the *effect* is that of the narrator addressing a character. It is this effect that Lorca produces and I include non-narrator apostrophes in my comparisons. I know of no traditional *romance* in which, as in Lorca (*RG* 7:9–38, 12:37–40), a character addresses the narrator. Here as elsewhere Lorca develops his *romance* inheritance rather than merely accepting it.

the parallelistic interplay of similarities and contrasts:

Yo me quité la corbata.	Cf. vos venís en gruesa mula,
Ella se quitó el vestido.	yo en ligero caballo;
Yo el cinturón con revólver.	vos traéis sayo de seda,
Ella sus cuatro corpiños (6:24–7).	yo traigo un arnés tranzado
	(*RVC* 16)

incantatory repetitions and play on repetitions:

¡Cuántas veces te esperó!	Cf. ¡Bien se te emplea, buen rey,
¡Cuántas veces te esperara!	buen rey, bien se te empleara!
(4:69–70)	(*RVC* 85a)

Several of the above are more characteristic of Lorca than of the medieval poet, most notably the predominant — and essentially dramatic — use of present tenses to evoke past action. In traditional *romances* expressive features of the type illustrated are commonly integrated into a firm, preterite-guided and at times even pedestrian narrative progression in which verb tenses, for example, may vary not for expressive purposes but in an apparently arbitrary fashion or simply because of rhyme needs (as in the line-filler variants, 'Bien oiréis lo que decía/dirá', 'Bien oiréis lo que hablaba/habló/ha hablado'). One has no such impression in Lorca's *romances*. Nor does one find as much intellectualising subordination as in certain traditional *romances*, or as many abstractions, or comparable disputes on love and valour and justice, or as much dependence on soft-centred emotive nouns and adjectives ('suspiros', 'gemidos'; 'valerosos brazos', 'honrados pechos') .... It is as though Lorca distilled from the traditional ballad its most expressive features — at least for twentieth-century tastes — and incorporated them into poems of wholly contemporary appeal. Two of these features stand out and have not so far been illustrated:

the use of hard imagery (here to create a death scene):

Un ángel marchoso pone	Cf. Doliente estaba, doliente,
su cabeza en un cojín.	ese buen rey don Fernando
Otros de rubor cansado	los pies tiene cara oriente
encendieron un candil (12:45–8)	y la candela en la mano
	(*RVC* 35)

and the exploitation of wider resonances (here suggesting cosmic involvement in human misfortune):

Espadón de nebulosa
mueve en el aire Santiago.
Grave silencio, de espalda,
manaba el cielo combado.

*

El veinticinco de junio
abrió sus ojos Amargo,
y el veinticinco de agosto
se tendió para cerrarlos
                    $(14:42-9)^5$

Cf. Los aires andan contrarios,
     el sol eclipse hacía,
     la luna perdió su lumbre,
     el norte no parecía,
     cuando el triste rey don Juan
     en su cama yacía,
     cercado de pensamientos,
     que valer no se podía
                    (*RVC* 98)

For the reader of today these are two of the most superbly evocative aspects of the early *romance*. But they are not frequent and most poems offer little or no evidence. In *Romancero gitano*, in contrast, any poem will serve to illustrate both points. On the one hand Lorca wants to make his *romance* 'trabado y sólido como una piedra' (III, 884); on the other hand he wants it to serve as a springboard to something far wider, 'misterioso e indescifrable' (III, 342). But no clear division is possible. The former pair of examples above emphasises the physical here-and-now; the latter, the wider resonances. But each is present in each. This is far more typical of *Romancero gitano*, than of traditional *romances*.

We are passing gradually from similarities to differences — of frequency, of emphasis, of subtlety of use .... A few further examples must suffice. Lorca, for example, writes not only as a poet but also as a dramatist, and reference has been made to his more frequent use of the present tense to bring persons and events close to us. One finds something similar in his emphasis on temporal and physical placing, in the overall structure and progression of his poems, and in his concern with character portrayal, especially self-revealing character portrayal. The following pair of examples will serve to illustrate this last point:

Yo me quité la corbata.
Ella se quitó el vestido.
Yo el cinturón con revólver.
Ella sus cuatro corpiños (6:24–7).

Cf. ellas quitan la su saya
     y yo el mi pantalón;
     ellas quitan su camisa,
     y yo el mi camisón (*35*, 65).

---

[5] On 25 June Amargo was warned that he would die within two months. Saint James, whose saint's day is at the mid-point, 25 July, seals the decree with his cosmic sword (*vía de Santiago, the Milky Way*) and the sky (also heaven) turns its back on Amargo. His death follows as announced.

In each case the braggart protagonist describes an amatory escapade, with traditional parallelism and interplay of similarities and contrasts. But Lorca's gypsy is more clearly characterised as a braggart because of an extra element of contrast: between his own modest undressing (tie and revolver) and the girl's more thorough and apparently enthusiastic stripping down (dress and four petticoats). His macho virility, he suggests, is conferred as a favour.

Lorca's immediately following lines illustrate a further difference from the traditional *romance*:

Ni nardos ni caracolas	Cf. Esta noche, caballeros,
tienen el cutis tan fino,	dormí con una doncella,
ni los cristales con luna	que en los días de mi vida
relumbran con ese brillo.	yo no vi cosa más bella.
(6:28–31)	(*RVC* 139)

In each case the girl's beauty is emphasised by its proclaimed superiority to an evoked element. But whereas the anonymous poet's evoked element is a simple, generic *cosa más bella*, Lorca creates the beauty for his reader by means of sense imagery. This too is characteristic of his writing and notably less characteristic of early traditional *romances*. His rich metaphorical language takes us but a step further (with a relatively rare traditional example for comparison):

	Cf. [The Cid would have seized
	all the Moorish kings]
Toda la alcoba sufría	mas poniendo a los pies alas,
con sus ojos llenos de alas	desembarazan la tierra.
(18:39–40)	(*RC* 84)

As Pedro Salinas observed, we are here touching on the most notable distinguishing feature of Lorca's *romance* style:

> Su obra de romancista, en cuanto a técnica, podría definirse como la saturación del cuerpo entero del romance por el espíritu metafórico, por la metáfora. Ningún poeta se ha lanzado sobre la simple textura del romance con tal ansia de metaforizarla hasta lo hondo. Vivió Lorca en época en que la metáfora se declaró reina del lenguaje poético, si bien hubo de renunciar pronto a sus insensatas pretensiones. Pero él comprendió que las imágenes no son exorno o arreo, sino cuerpo mismo donde encarna la poesía, y dio al romance carne de metáfora (*19*, 351).

Illustrations were offered earlier (under 'Pruning the Lyrical Tree')
and I here confine myself to a single further example, using it also to
suggest yet another difference between Lorca's *romances* and those of
the Middle Ages:

Las piquetas de los gallos	Cf. Media noche era por filo,
cavan buscando la aurora,	los gallos querían cantar,
cuando por el monte oscuro	conde Claros con amores
baja Soledad Montoya (7:1–4).	no podía reposar (*RVC* 190).

In each quotation the appearance of the protagonist is accompanied by
brief temporal and physical scene-setting, and the juxtaposition, in the
traditional *romance* of midnight, approaching cockcrows and the sleep-
less, lovelorn Conde Claros sets up magical resonances. But there is
greater sophistication in Lorca's lines and reference was made earlier
to the metaphor and synaesthesia in lines 1–2. Moreover, in Lorca's
poems it is not so much the images themselves that are important as
their function in the overall context. The synaesthetic presentation of
the cockcrows (sound) as digging (sight) in search of the dawn, besides
suggesting the physical density of the darkness, introduces the theme
of attempted escape from darkness that will run through the poem.
And in lines 3–4 the name of the protagonist, besides being typically
gypsy, associates her both with the dark mountain (*monte/Montoya*)
and with the emotive darkness of her own loneliness (*Soledad*) and
suggests that she too is looking for a new dawn. In Lorca's poem, then,
there is a closer integration and interaction of elements than in the
traditional *romance* and the title of the poem is relevant to both setting
and protagonist. Not all this is immediately apparent. Lorca, like
others of his generation, emphasised the need for conscious effort in
poetry, by both writer and reader, and there is much conscious elabo-
ration in these lines. But expression could hardly be more concise. And
there is enough simplicity and immediate appeal to hold one's interest
while more mysterious and subtle resonances make their impact
increasingly with each successive reading. One can say something
similar of the latent mystery of *cerrados* in the opening *Coches cerrados
llegaban / a las orillas de juncos* (9:1–2), of the magic in *La luna vino a
la fragua / con su polisón de nardos* (1:1–2), of the cosmic resonances
in *Su luna de pergamino / Preciosa tocando viene* (2:1–2), of the epic
character build-up in the opening of the 'Prendimiento ...' (11:1–4).
Immediate appeal prompts interest and involvement; less easily defin-
able resonances gradually create a more potent dynamism that carries

the reader on, even through images that he may not understand, to a fuller enjoyment and appreciation of Lorca's poetry. With his starting-point in the simplicity and directness of the *romance* Lorca raises his poems to a complexity and intensity of resonances that the traditional *romance* itself rarely, if ever, attains.

The Five Senses

Alongside a profusion of stylistic features that are characteristic of traditional *romances* the last paragraphs point to a number of differences, at least of emphasis: a more dramatic approach to what is narrated, with greater emphasis on scene-placing and character portrayal; a more direct evocation of beauty, for example, so that the reader experiences it for himself (*Ni nardos ni caracolas / tienen el cutis tan fino ...*) instead of being merely told about it (*cosa más bella*); finally and especially, a far more frequent and wide-ranging use of metaphor. Underlying these differences is Lorca's notably greater emphasis on sense perceptions. The poet, said Lorca, 'tiene que ser profesor en los cinco sentidos corporales. Los cinco sentidos corporales, en este orden: vista, tacto, oído, olfato y gusto' (III, 229). In fact, sound is more frequent than touch in *Romancero gitano*, but for the rest Lorca here points to one of the work's most striking features. Opening lines will serve as an initial illustration. In *La luna vino a la fragua / con su polisón de nardos* (1:1–2) simple appearance on scene (*vino*) is accompanied by essential placing (*fragua*), as in traditional *romances*, but also by less traditional visualisation of the personified moon; in *Su luna de pergamino / Preciosa tocando viene* (2:1–2) simple appearance (*viene*) is accompanied by the visual evocation of the girl's tambourine (*luna de pergamino*) and an associated reference to touch and sound (*tocando*); in *En la mitad del barranco / las navajas de Albacete, / bellas de sangre contraria, / relucen como los peces* (3:1–4), simple traditional placing (*En la mitad del barranco*) is followed by less traditional emphasis on visual effects .... One could continue in similar fashion through the book. *Venir*, with its indication of a character's appearance or progress, is the most frequently used verb in *Romancero gitano*. But in line with the poet's emphasis on the senses it is followed closely in frequency by verbs of perception, most notably *ver* and *mirar*. As the following table shows, other sense elements too are strikingly present:

sense perceptions	*stimuli to sense perception*
ver, mirar	relucir, relumbrar, brillar ...; profiles, colours,

blood, flower imagery . . . ; *Vuelan en la araña gris /
siete pájaros del prisma* (5:5–6).

sentir (*to hear*) cantar, sonar, tocar (*to play*) . . . ; rumores, gritos,
silencio . . . ; *el mar bate y canta* (2:7); *rumor de
viejas voces / resonaba* (13:20–1).

tocar (*to touch*) morder, clavar, frío, caliente, duro, agudo . . . ; *un
norte / de metales y peñascos* (14:10–11); *Son tus
besos en mi espalda / avispas y vientecillos* (18:
62–3).

[oler] oler, olor, endulzar . . . ; *huele a caballo y a sombra*
(7:6); *fragante de agua colonia* (8:27); *un olor de
vino y ámbar* (13–17).

gustar (*to taste*) amargo, agrio, dulce, salobre, zumo de limón,
azúcar . . . ; *dejaba / en la boca un raro gusto / de
hiel, de menta y de albahaca* (4:64–6).

In many cases, including some of the above, it is difficult to categorise
the sense with certainly — *salobre* (8:8), for example, suggests both the
smell and the taste of the air — and in others there is a clear synaesthe-
tic superposition of different senses, as in *senos de duro estaño* (1:8;
sight and touch), *un horizonte de perros / ladra muy lejos del río* (6:18–
19; sight and sound), *al son de panderos fríos* (18:15; sound and touch)
and *La higuera frota su viento / con la lija de sus ramas* (4:17–18; sight,
sound and touch). Also, like other aspects of the here-and-now, sense
perceptions in Lorca commonly have wider resonances. *Senos de duro
estaño*, for example, in context, is not merely sensorial; beyond the
evocation of sight and touch it suggests also, with its tacit contrast to the
comforting maternal breast, emotional detachment and inaccessibility.
We shall return to such resonances in a later section. For the moment
our concern is with the senses themselves. The effect of so much em-
phasis on them is to bring protagonist, setting and action close to the
reader and thereby to increase the immediacy of impact. In the work's
immediacy of impact lies also its immediacy of appeal.[6] 'La casada
infiel', with its interplay of senses and sensuality, offers a profusion of

[6] The above indications take on greater significance in the light of Víctor
García Hoz's findings (*Vocabulario usual, común y fundamental*, Madrid
1953). Basing himself on a wide range and variety of Spanish texts García
Hoz finds the following to be the ten most frequent verbs (I indicate in

examples (notably in lines 6–19) that are both revealing and easily accessible to the first-time reader.

In a section on Lorca's appeal to the senses reference must be made, finally, to the music of his lines. It is another aspect of his writing in which he echoes traditional *romances* (cf. above, p. 22) but goes further than most, with echoes especially of shorter-lined, more song-like *romancillos*:

Verde que te quiero verde.	Cf. A la verde, verde,
Verde viento. Verdes ramas.	a la verde oliva.
(4:1–2)	(*RVC* III, 176)
Dejando un rastro de sangre.	Ya le llevan a la reina,
Dejando un rastro de lágrimas.	ya se lo van a llevar.
(4:55–6)	(*RVC* 195)
¡Ay San Gabriel de mis ojos!	Madre, la mi madre,
¡Gabrielillo de mi vida!	la mi siempre amiga.
(10:47–8)	(*RVC* III, 178)
en la noche platinoche,	Que con el aretín,
noche que noche nochera.	que con el aretón.
(15:35–6)	(*RVC* III, 179)

With Lorca's last lines above one can compare also the well-known children's rhyme 'Luna lunera, / cascabelera' (cf. Lorca's use elsewhere of 'luna lunera', I, 28, 725). But as with other imagery, snippet

square brackets the corresponding figures for *Romancero gitano*): *ser* (7130 occurrences [22]), *haber* (4646 [11]), *estar* (2028 [16]), *tener* (1833 [13]), *hacer* (1777 [4]), *decir* (1649 [9]), *poder* (1381 [5]), *ir* (1155 [10]), *dar* (1020 [9]), *ver* (925 [14]). In *Romancero gitano* the ten most frequent verbs (with bracketed García Hoz findings) are: *venir* (24 [496]), *ser* (22 [7130]), *estar* (16 [2028]), *ver* (14 [925]), *querer* (14 [634]), *dejar* (13 [312]), *tener* (13 [1833]), *cantar* (13 [53]), *mirar* (12 [96]), *haber* (11 [4646]). A number of points stand out: Lorca's relatively infrequent use of *ser* and *estar* (since he tends to omit mere link words, leaving the sentence without a verb, often as an exclamation) and of *haber* (since his emphasis is on the present); the comparable frequency of *tener* (which therefore has no significance); Lorca's strikingly frequent use of *venir* (usually to indicate a character's appearance or progress), of *ver* and *mirar* (visual perception), of *cantar* (stimulus to auditory perception, usually suggesting vitality) and of *querer* and *dejar* (expressions of desire). In these few words one is not far from a synthesis of *Romancero gitano*.

quotation like the above is unsatisfactory. Effects have to be seen in context. 'Romance de la luna, luna', with its incantatory, almost hypnotic impact, merits the reader's attention as an especially fine example of significant musicality.

ROMANCERO GITANO: THE WIDER RESONANCES

At the beginning of the previous section I likened Lorca's poetry and its impact to that of a stone thrown into a pond: at the centre, the specific point of impact ('forma', 'núcleo central'); around it, widening circles of resonance and significance ('radio de acción', 'redonda perspectiva'). My emphasis so far has been on the point of impact, 'el elemento que pudiéramos llamar realista, aunque no lo es' (III, 342): characters, conflicts, settings, props; sense perceptions; the hard centre of Lorca's imagery — all aided by the directness and vividness of traditional *romance* style. Lorca himself emphasised the importance of this generally more accessible aspect of his writing: 'Quiero conseguir que las imágenes que hago sobre los tipos sean *entendidas* por estos, sean visiones del mundo que viven, y de esta manera hacer el romance *trabado* y sólido como una piedra' (III, 884). Ezra Pound had made a similar point in the article referred to earlier; 'I believe that the proper and perfect symbol is the natural object, that if a man use "symbols" he must so use them that their symbolic function does not obtrude; so that *a* sense, and the poetic quality of the passage, is not lost to those who do not understand the symbol as such, to whom, for instance, a hawk is a hawk'. So far, then, the hard centre, 'sólido como una piedra', accessible to those for whom 'a hawk is a hawk'; henceforth, the wider resonances, the 'radio de acción', the 'redonda perspectiva'. The following short poem from *Canciones* (1927) will serve to indicate the transition (with my own letters alongside the poem to aid commentary):

> *Nocturno esquemático*
>
> | Hinojo, serpiente y junco. | A^1, B^1 y C^1 |
> | Aroma, rastro y penumbra. | A^2, B^2 y C^2 |
> | Aire, tierra y soledad. | A^3, B^3 y C^3 |
> | (La escala llega a la luna.) (I, 274) | |

Starting from specific objects (line 1), the poem moves progressively outwards to associated resonances, at first fairly immediate (line 2), then wider (line 3). Moreover, guided by the clear progression in A^1, A^2, A^3 (fennel that leaves its scent on the air) and B^1, B^2, B^3 (a snake that leaves its track on the earth), the reader is encouraged to find a similar and more significant emotive progression in C^1, C^2, C^3 (reeds that create half-light — and mystery — and a sense of solitude). In his final line Lorca himself points to the widened 'radio de acción': 'La escala llega a la luna', that is, to an emotive realm of magic and mystery.

Character Enhancement

In 'San Gabriel (Sevilla)' Lorca offers a neo-primitive gypsy version of the biblical Annunciation (Luke 1:26–38). It is the most charming and jauntily seductive poem in the book. In the opening lines a handsome youth roams the streets of Seville. We shall return later to the sort of stylisation exemplified in lines 1–10. For the moment it almost suffices to note that the imagery is non-realistic and that it thus serves to distance both poem and protagonist from ordinary prosaic reality. But line 6 is important in another respect too, for the descriptive build-up of lines 1–5 is here resolved in action (*ronda la desierta calle*) that echoes the most famous of *sevillanas* ('Ronda mi calle'). The effect is to elevate the *bello niño de junco* and his action to almost archetypal *sevillano* status (cf. later *biznieto de la Giralda*, 33). I find similar elevation in the following lines:

> En la ribera del mar
> no hay palma que se le iguale,
> ni emperador coronado,
> ni lucero caminante.
> 15 Cuando la cabeza inclina
> sobre su pecho de jaspe,
> la noche busca llanuras
> porque quiere arrodillarse.
> Las guitarras suenan solas
> 20 para San Gabriel Arcángel,
> domador de palomillas
> y enemigo de los sauces (10:11–22).

On the whole seashore (with a sense of vastness and uplift in the poem's departure from the more ordinary *A orillas del mar*) there is no palm tree his equal (with a suggestion of elegance and an echo of palms of glory and triumph), nor crowned emperor nor wandering star (both frequent in Andalusian speech and song as pointers to status and illusion).[1] Having elevated his protagonist by measurement against — and proclaimed superiority to — successive elements of distinction, Lorca proceeds to elevate him further by evidence of homage from the world around: first, personified night (17–18); then, guitars stirred to life as if by magic (19). It is at this point that the full name and title first appear: *San Gabriel Arcángel* (20). *Domador* in the following line is normally associated with unbroken horses or wild animals, but the annunciating archangel is here a tamer of little doves, suggesting gentleness but also recalling innumerable early paintings of the Annunciation where doves represent the descent of the Holy Spirit. Since willows are associated with lamentation and Saint Gabriel brings glad tidings, he is naturally *enemigo de los sauces* (22).

The range of Lorca's enhancement techniques is already impressive: stylising dissociation from crude reality (throughout), an echo of *cante* (*ronda la desierta calle*), subtle exploitation of the Spanish linguistic system (*En la ribera del mar* rather than *A orillas del mar*), popular and biblical resonances (*palma, emperador, lucero*), the homage of the world around (*noche, guitarras*), an echo of Christian iconography and of early paintings (*palomillas* and the central action of the poem). At this point the narrator, anxious that the 'highly favoured' virgin should be a gypsy girl, reminds the archangel of his debt to the gypsies: *No olvides que los gitanos/te regalaron el traje*, a reference to the clothing of his statue in the local church. After so much elevation this brings us back close to real-life normality and Part II opens with the appearance of Anunciación:

> Anunciación de los Reyes,
> bien lunada y mal vestida,
> abre la puerta al lucero
> que por la calle venía (10:27–30).

Mal vestida, abre la puerta and *por la calle* keep us close to reality. But there is elevation too, initially in the name: *Anunciación* associates the girl immediately with her unique destiny, *Reyes* is a typical gypsy surname that serves to emphasise her lineage, and the whole resonant and regal-sounding name suggests distinction and nobility. Anunciación is no ordinary gypsy girl, it seems. The implication already is that she is

---

[1] Here as elsewhere, fuller justification is offered in my volume of commentaries.

blessed among gypsy women. But there is more to the name than this. In seeking to explain Lorca's association of Saint Gabriel with Seville critics have suggested that he is the city's patron saint and that it is his statue that looks out from the pinnacle of the Giralda. Both these suggestions are mistaken. The statue on the Giralda tower is the Giraldillo, a bronze female figure representing Faith, and Seville's patron saint — strictly, the patron saint of the archdiocese of Seville — is Nuestra Señora de los Reyes. It is the latter point that is here important. Anunciación's name serves not only to associate her with her destiny of highly favoured motherhood and to emphasise her gypsy lineage; it also identifies her with Seville's patron saint and associates her with the Virgin Mary at the moment of her own Annunciation. Moreover, like Saint Gabriel, Anunciación is further exalted by the echoing of Andalusian *cante*, this time one of the best known of traditional *peteneras*:

> ¿Dónde vas, linda gitana,
> tan compuesta y tan bonita?
> Voy en busca de un lucero
> que el sentío a mí me quita.

The similarity to the quoted four-line presentation of Anunciación is striking and surely not fortuitous. One notices, first, the same assonance in *í-a* (to which Lorca has just changed after the presentation of Saint Gabriel with *a-e* assonance), secondly, the similarly structured second line (adverb-adjective *y* adverb-adjective), and thirdly, the word *lucero* which occupies the same final position in both third lines and serves as a similar image of illusion. The consequence of these various *petenera* resonances in Lorca's lines is to bring the remaining elements closer together. In the first line the parallel of *Anunciación de los Reyes* and *linda gitana* serves to reinforce Anunciación's gypsiness and to make of her, more clearly still, the archetypal *linda gitana*, and in the last two lines the intoxication of *el sentío a mí me quita* is carried over to suggest Anunciación's own bewildered response to her herald of good tidings. Lorca's lines, then, both echo the *petenera* and gain strength from it. The gained strength involves an increased impression of stature, of typical gypsiness, of significance and of universality. Immediacy is still important, but now it has transcendental overtones. As in lines 29–30 (*abre la puerta al lucero / que por la calle venía*) domestic realism can henceforth mingle appropriately with cosmic symbol. And it does — throughout the rest of the poem.

'San Gabriel' is succeeded by the two Antoñito poems. The first, 'Prendimiento de Antoñito el Camborio en el camino de Sevilla', tells of a gypsy's arrest by the Civil Guard; the second, 'Muerte de Antoñito el Camborio', tells of his murder by fellow gypsies. As in the presentation of Anunciación the opening lines make immediately clear that Antoñito is no ordinary gypsy:

> Antonio Torres Heredia,
> hijo y nieto de Camborios,
> con una vara de mimbre
> va a Sevilla a ver los toros (11:1–4).

Antonio, *Torres* and *Heredia* are all typical gypsy names and *Torres* has resonances of *tower* of strength, an effect that is reinforced by the repeated stressed *o* and the stately rhythm of the line. The effect is pressed home in the following line where Lorca declares openly what we should already have felt: that Antonio Torres Heredia is a thoroughbred gypsy, *hijo y nieto de Camborios* (with another stressed *o* that reinforces the effect of *Antonio Torres*). Amidst so much elevation of tone the *vara* of line 3 suggests a staff of office or authority ('vara de alcalde', 'vara de juez') but proves to be a pliant willow switch, with the implication of easy acceptance of nobility by a correspondingly pliant, easy-going character. After so much build-up the release comes finally in line 4 with the appearance, at last, of the verb and the almost casual, throwaway indication of the object of Antoñito's journey. But here too the elements are carefully chosen: Lorca's gypsy of gypsies is appropriately associated with Seville, the Andalusian city of fiestas *par excellence*, and with *the* Andalusian fiesta of fiestas, the bullfight. Every element, then, besides individualising, serves also to epitomise. Antonio is clearly no commonplace gypsy. By the manner of his presentation (as in the presentation of Anunciación) Lorca has made of him the incarnation of all gypsies in what he most esteems in them: 'lo más elevado, lo más profundo, más aristocrático de mi país, lo más representativo de su modo y el que guarda el ascua, la sangre y el alfabeto de la verdad andaluza y universal' (III, 342). If Lorca can here be described as a gypsy poet, it is not in a realistic sense. By the subtle and expressive use of language he has made of Antoñito an archetypal gypsy of his own vision and creation.

But there is more to the lines than this. In the presentation of Saint Gabriel and Anunciación we saw how Lorca's lines gained strength from their echoing of Andalusian *cante*. In the present case they gain

strength from another traditional art form, the *romance morisco*. To
illustrate this I quote extracts from two such *romances*:

Celín, señor de Escariche,	Zulema, al fin, el valiente,
y Aliatar, Rey de Granada,	hijo del fuerte Zulema [. . .],
Azarques y Abenhumeyas	fue a ver en Avila un día
salen a juego de cañas.	las fiestas como de fiesta.
(*RGen* 630)	(*RGen* 700)

Noble heroes, resonant names, proud lineage, festive activities, *cante*-
like build-up and release of tension, the use of four-line periods (in
contrast to the more purely narrative Castilian *romance* where two-line
periods predominate) — these are some of the most notable charac-
teristics of *romances moriscos* that are echoed in the opening lines
of the 'Prendimiento'. And to these basic similarities can be added,
also in Lorca's opening lines, Antoñito's character-revealing *vara de
mimbre* which recalls the *morisco* hero in festive mood: '[El Tarfe] sólo
lleva por empresa / un verde ramo apazible' (*RGen* 137); 'La gruesa
lança de fresno / parece en sus manos mimbre' (*RGen* 657). The conse-
quence of so many *romance* resonances is that, to the adequately pre-
pared reader, Antoñito appears not only as the epitome of the noble
gypsy of the present but also as the epitome of the noble hero of
Spain's epic and ballad past.

Antoñito, then, is elevated to archetypal gypsy and archetypal hero.
But there is yet more elevation and again the similarity to Lorca's
presentation of Anunciación is striking. The title of the poem, with its
unusual use of the word *prendimiento*, has resonances of the 'taking' of
Christ, much represented in Holy Week tableaux (as in the 'Sagrado
Prendimiento de Nuestro Señor Jesucristo' in Seville), and of His road
to Calvary (as in Raphael's 'Caída en el camino del Calvario' in the
Madrid Prado). Nor is it the title alone. The *vara de mimbre* may con-
ceivably recall the Passion of Christ — and several Holy Week tableaux
— where 'they put [. . .] a reed in his right hand' and mocked him as
King of the Jews (Matthew 27:29); more certainly, the *cinco tricornios*
(28), with a number that has mystified critics, recall the five civil guards
who, when there is no resident military garrison or naval base, tradi-
tionally form the Holy Week escort for the tableau of Christ (one at
each corner and the corporal behind); the repeated *nueve de la noche*
(39, 43) echoes the biblical 'ninth hour' when 'Jesus cried out with a
loud voice, saying Eli, Eli, lama sabachthani? that is to say, My God,
my God, why hast thou forsaken me?' (Matthew 27:46); the proclaimed
killing of Antoñito out of envy in the following poem (12:27–8) recalls

the biblical words 'For he knew that for envy they had delivered him' (Matthew 27:18), and the presence of angels at Antoñito's death (12: 45–8) is in line with countless fifteenth-century paintings where angels are present at Christ's crucifixion. Antoñito, then, has not only been elevated to archetypal gypsy (resonant names and noble lineage) and archetypal hero (echoes of ballad literature). Because of the indicated pointers to the Passion of Christ he is also the archetypal man of good (cf. Lorca's own description of him as 'gitano verdadero, incapaz del mal', III, 345). He submits meekly to arrest and, like Christ, suffers from his submission: injustice of his enemies, incomprehension of his friends, loneliness in suffering. The Camborio who in real life, it seems, was a drunken gypsy horse-dealer has been elevated and universalised by means of a series of skilfully wrought resonances that the reader perceives only vaguely, almost subconsciously, according to his sensitivity to language and his awareness of the cultural traditions in which Lorca himself was immersed.

There are other elements of enhancement, too, in the development of the Antoñito poems: further echoes of ballad literature; the involvement of nature which in lines 17–24 of the 'Prendimiento' takes over as the main protagonist, echoing Antoñito's own earlier actions, recalling the fiesta that he was hoping to see and pointing to the possibility of escape from his captors; the relating of Antoñito's destiny to the cosmic *noche de Capricornio* (22); tacit contrasts with the debased civil guards (28, 41–2); the presentation of the gypsy's arrest and imprisonment with resonances of a Greek tragedy, in three acts (1–16, 17–28, 39–46) with chorus (29–38). All these things serve to elevate and universalise the action of the 'Prendimiento' and the process continues in the following poem where Antoñito's meekness finally erupts into almost cosmic wrath, with an epic fight, the further involvement of nature, another mini-tragedy with chorus, and the final death, appropriately attended by biblical angels. If the reader finds in the *tres golpes de sangre* of which Antoñito dies a significant echo of the *tres clavos* and *tres heridas* and *tres balas de almendra verde* of the Annunciation poem — and of the traditional three nails of Christ's crucifixion —, he will surely not be mistaken. Such echoes are one of the reasons for the powerful impact of Lorca's poetry.

The Springboard of the Senses

Character enhancement is only a small part of a wider phenomenon. It has here been studied separately in order to illustrate an aspect of

Lorca's writing that has been somewhat neglected. Numerous critics have pointed to echoes of the traditional *romance*, some have pointed also to echoes of *cante* and yet others to iconographical and biblical resonances. But what is important is not the presence of such resonances but the reason for their presence, what they contribute, in context, to Lorca's own poetry. His technique of character enhancement offers a partial answer: echoes of *romance*, *cante*, bible and Christian iconography add stature and significance. But as the commented examples show, it is not only echoes from outside the poem that produce this effect; the interplay of words, sounds and rhythms within the poem is important too. And protagonists are not only elevated by such techniques; they are also characterised (Antoñito, for example, as both hero and man of peace). Finally, wider resonances are relevant not only to characters but also to actions and settings (cf. comments in the concluding paragraph above). Despite the poet's emphasis on sense perceptions there is no realism in *Romancero gitano* and perhaps no line without resonances beyond the literal surface meaning of the words used.

At the simplest level one finds lines such as the following:

> —Compadre, quiero cambiar
> mi caballo por su casa,
> mi montura por su espejo,
> mi cuchillo por su manta (4:25–8).

Two series are set in contrast to one another: *caballo*, *montura*, *cuchillo*, suggesting a macho life of freedom and danger, and *casa*, *espejo*, *manta*, suggesting a settled life of domesticity and security. 'Go in fear of abstractions,' said Pound. Like others of his generation, Lorca seeks not to 'abstract' but to present relevant physical phenomena so that the reader can experience them directly and infer for himself what lies behind. It is characteristic of so-called 'hard imagery'. The following lines are similar, but with mini-scenes instead of separate physical objects:

> ¡Se acabaron los gitanos
> que iban por el monte solos!
> Están los viejos cuchillos
> tiritando bajo el polvo (11:35–8).

Gypsy valour is no more and the gypsies of the past are enraged [at this], with the bracketed 'at this' as a reminder that Lorca suggests rather than states causality, again exposing his reader to the evidence but not seeking to interpret it for him.

At times, as in the examples given of character enhancement, understanding and impact depend in part on the reader's awareness of a reference to something outside the poem. This may be an aspect of popular culture, as in the following, which echoes a gypsy wedding rite to test the bride's virginity and thereby points to Thamar's own lost virginity:

> Paños blancos, enrojecen
> en las alcobas cerradas (18:89–90)

Or it may be something as sophisticated and elitest as the poetry of Góngora, with a dozen or more pointers in a single poem (significantly 'San Rafael', the poem dedicated to Góngora's native Cordoba) and even a hidden hendecasyllable with typical Gongorine antithesis and mirror symmetry:

> ... dora el agua
> y los mármoles enluta (9:39–40).

At other times the resonance is dependent solely on the immediate context, as in the following aphoristic pointer to the danger of giving way to passion:

> —Soledad de mis pesares,
> caballo que se desboca,
> al fin encuentra la mar
> y se lo tragan las olas (7:15–18),

and in the following indication of transition from the world of man to the world of nature:

> Se apagaron los faroles
> y se encendieron los grillos (6:6–7).

Between these extremes of dependence on resonances from outside the poem and imagistic self-sufficiency, the transition from 'núcleo central' to 'redonda perspectiva' most commonly depends on the overall context of the poem itself and is fully appreciated only in that context:

> Antonio Torres Heredia,
> hijo y nieto de Camborios,
> viene sin vara de mimbre
> entre los cinco tricornios (11:25–8).

Except for the metonymic *tricornios* the third and fourth lines seem, out of context, to be straightforward realistic description. But the opening four lines of the poem are still echoing within us and lines 25–6 remind us of them with repetition of the epic lines 1–2. Thereafter, all is contrast: *con una vara de mimbre* has given way to *sin vara de mimbre*, outward-looking *va . . . a ver* to confined *viene entre*, noble *toros* to debased *tricornios*, similarly horned but in a very different sense. Viewed in context, this apparently realistic description epitomises Antoñito's upturned fortunes. Similar examples abound in every poem but have been generally neglected by critics, at times with resulting misinterpretation. I illustrate this in my companion volume and here confine myself to a number of opening descriptions. Reference was made earlier to the first lines of 'Romance de la pena negra'. The description, it was suggested, anticipates the central theme of the poem. One finds something similar elsewhere. Two of Lorca's most difficult *romances* will serve to illustrate the point.

'San Rafael (Córdoba)' starts with the arrival of carriages along the banks of the Guadalquivir:

> Coches cerrados llegaban
> a las orillas de juncos
> donde las ondas alisan
> romano torso desnudo (9:1–4).

It is possible to read this as realistic description, with even the *romano torso desnudo* seen as a limbless Roman statue. But the mystery of *coches cerrados* and uncontoured *orillas de juncos* contrasts with the firmer resonances of *donde las ondas* and sculpted Roman form (surely the city itself) and thus anticipates a duality that will gradually become clearer as the poem progresses:

> Blanda Córdoba de juncos.
> Córdoba de arquitectura (9:29–30).

This, in turn, is an image of a still more important duality, that of the city's two great ages and cultures: Moorish Cordoba, delicate and decorative, mysterious and magical, and Roman Cordoba, sculpted and architectural, resonant and triumphant. It is significantly *el Arcángel aljamiado*, Saint Raphael, and his iconographically inseparable fish who join the two Cordobas in harmony. In the apparently realistic opening lines Lorca again anticipated the central theme of his poem.

'Thamar y Amnón' is probably the most densely written and most

difficult poem in the book. As in 'San Rafael', the opening lines anti-
cipate the rest and I aim to show this. But I wish to illustrate, at the
same time, a further aspect of Lorca's wider resonances and point to an
area of critical disagreement: that of his imagery. As a preliminary I
take a less difficult example of imagery from elsewhere in the book —
Yunques ahumados sus pechos, / gimen canciones redondas (7:7–8) —
and concentrate on the first line. The image consists of a real plane
(*pechos*) and an evoked plane (*yunques ahumados*) and both are pre-
sent within the poem. Two things especially are notable: first, that the
evoked plane is not subordinated to the real plane (as it would be, for
example, if Lorca had written 'Sus pechos, yunques ahumados, gimen
. . .'); it makes its impact in initial position, before the real plane has
been declared; secondly, that the comma after *pechos* helps to fuse
evoked plane and real plane and invites the reader to tarry over the
fusion and feel the resonances before proceeding further. Both these
things tend to exalt the evoked plane and to give it special importance.
Elsewhere — and notably in the opening lines of 'Thamar y Amnón' —
Lorca gives even greater importance to the evoked plane by omitting
the real plane and leaving the reader to infer it. It is here especially that
critical disagreements may appear. But the poet does not omit the real
plane merely to tease or mystify his reader. His aim is to give relevant
free play to the resonances of his evoked plane, unrestricted by any
specific real-life equation. With this in mind, I invite the reader to
consider the first section of 'Thamar y Amnón' (18:1–12). The moon
turns over the parched lands while summer sows murmurs of tiger and
flame (1–4). There is no question here, as there was at the beginning of
'San Rafael', of realistic description, but the imagery is notably sense-
based and it serves again as a springboard to wider resonances. In *el
verano siembra / rumores de tigre y llama* (3–4) critics have found
pointers to the thunder and lightning of an approaching storm (real
plane) and this may well be justified. But other resonances are more
important in context. On the one hand, in the moon's turning, there is
a suggestion of distance and detachment, perhaps also of infertility
since the moon is traditionally associated with the bringing of rain and
here there is no rain; on the other hand, in the summer's sowing, there
is closeness and involvement, with suggestions of potential fertility (cf.
siembra) represented by rumblings, untamed animal and flame (all
recurrent Lorcan images of vitality). The duality will be developed
throughout the poem: centrally in the figures of the detached, lunar
Thamar and the passionate, earthy Amnón, but also in the surrounding

world of nature. The emotive resonances of *verano*, *siembra*, *rumores*, *tigre* and *llama* are clearly more relevant to this than mere thunder and lightning. Similarly in the immediately following lines: *Por encima de los techos / nervios de metal sonaban* (5–6). The image has apparently mystified critics and only Hernández attempts an explanation, interpreting the *nervios de metal* as lightning (*4*, 33). But in context, it seems, the image's most immediate function is to suggest steely sinews, between heaven (the realm of the moon) and earth (the realm of the tiger), as though bracing the universe in tension and harmony. There is also a more specific — though for the moment less important — physical reference, but not to lightning, and Lorca himself offers the key, in lines from another poem: 'El arpa y su lamento / prendido en nervios de metal dorado' (I, 959). The *nervios de metal*, then, are the strings of a harp and they will significantly be cut at the end of 'Thamar y Amnón'. But cut harp strings bring us back to the more emotive resonances of lines 5–6, for by the end of the poem cosmic harmony itself has been shattered. For external confirmation of Lorca's association of harp strings with cosmic harmony I merely point out that the above quoted poem (I, 958–9) is dedicated to the poet of cosmic harmony, Fray Luis de León. I continue with 'Thamar y Amnón: *Aire rizado venía / con los balidos de lana* (7–8). Like Hernández on the previous lines so López Castellón on these emphasises a physical justification for the image: 'El autor logra un efecto acertadísimo: aplica al aire el rizado del pelo de las ovejas, y a los balidos de éstas lo cálido de su lana' (*58*, 22). It is possible but not necessary to assume this. As in *aire conmovido* (1:5) the justification for *aire rizado* could be purely emotive. In *Poema del cante jondo*, for example, Lorca used the same image ('Se riza el aire gris', I, 157) — together with trembling reed, half light and cry-laden olive trees — as an appropriate setting for the most tragic of Andalusian *cantes*, the *siguiriya*. But there were no sheep present to support a physical explanation of *riza*; the rippled air was wholly emotive. *Rizado* in 'Thamar y Amnón', I suggest, is similar: it needs no physical justification; the sheep are there not to explain *rizado* but, with emotive relevance again, for their plaintive bleating over the barren earth. I conclude with the last four lines (9–12) and note only two points: first, that the earth 'offers itself' as though in sexual surrender; secondly, that its offer is accompanied by wounds (cf. earlier *tigre*) and cauteries of white light (cf. earlier *llama*). Thamar and Amnón have still not appeared, but we are in touch already with the central theme of the poem.

We have come a long way from mere emphasis on the senses. In the context of a Lorcan *romance* vividly presented elements of the real world and images composed of such elements become springboards to something far wider: character, themes, emotions, conflicts, mysterious forces . . . . Symbolism, in so far as it emphasises indefinable emotions, is too narrow a term, but there is much evidence of stylistic devices beloved of the Symbolists, and synaesthesia and musicality, referred to in earlier pages, are two of the most notable. I conclude the present section with a brief reference to another, colour symbolism. As is well known, colours do not merely indicate sense perceptions. Traditionally they may also have emotive resonances: black, grief; white, purity; red, passion; green, hope . . . . The use of colours in this traditional sense is commonly referred to as emblematic and there are examples in *Romancero gitano* (for example, the emblematic association of black and grief that underlies 'Romance de la pena negra'). But in the context of Lorca's poetry one must be wary of over-emphasis on simple equations. Green, says one critic, is the colour of youth and life; green, says another, is a symbol of bitter fate.[2] And each offers convincing evidence. But even in everyday usage colours have different emotive resonances according to the contexts in which they are used. Substitution illustrates the point: green grass, for example, suggests fresh grass (that is, something pleasant); green almonds, on the other hand, suggest bitter almonds (that is, something unpleasant). It is a feature of language that Lorca, with his sensitivity both to sense perceptions and to the interplay of words in context, exploits throughout his writing, and I have studied the duality elsewhere with reference to his use of red (life and death), white (purity and sterility) and yellow (prosperity and death) in *Bodas de sangre*. I here illustrate the duality further with reference to the colour green as used in a single poem, 'Romance

[2] 'verde — *juventud, vida*' (*17*, 152); 'La couleur verte [. . .] symbole d'amère fatalité' (*14*, 50). One finds similar polarisation with other colours, most notably yellow, which has been seen by some critics as a symbol of ill omen and by others as a symbol of optimism. In fact it can be both. As Lorca said of honey (in an early poem), it is illusion and suffering, summer and autumn, 'es la hoja marchita y es el trigo':

El que te gusta no sabe que traga
un resumen dorado del lirismo (I, 38).

In this, precisely, lies the key to Lorca's colour symbolism.

sonámbulo'. In the opening lines green appears as an object of longing, with suggestions of life, freshness and freedom, and everything in its proper place:

> Verde que te quiero verde.
> Verde viento. Verdes ramas.
> El barco sobre la mar
> y el caballo en la montaña (4:1–4).

But the appearance of the girl in the following lines denies the poet's longing with suggestions of withdrawal from life (*sombra*; *sueña*; *ojos de fría plata*) and *verde* here is no longer the colour of freshness but the colour of putrefaction (*verde carne, pelo verde*). Now the repeated opening line (9) is more forlorn. The clamour for green as life is threatened by contradictory resonances of green as death. Under the gypsy moon, the physical cause of the colour green in line 7 but also, more importantly, the malevolent source of the accompanying death associations, objects seem more alive than the girl herself. Again the poet affirms his longing for green and again his longing is denied, this time by the surrounding world of nature. For the coming dawn is not green. Instead it appears in shimmers of cold white against the surrounding darkness (*estrellas de escarcha*; *pez de sombra*). And the fig-tree, with a suggestion of dryness rather than freshness, grates its tamed wind (not the fresh, free *verde viento*) with the sandpaper of its branches (very different from the longed for *verdes ramas*). It is the basic duality of the poem: on the one hand, what is longed for; on the other hand, what life offers. The dialogue that follows develops the point and the repeated first two lines (61–2) echo even more forlornly amidst the accompanying disillusion and suffering, with no evidence that the speakers attain the longed for *altas barandas*, but with a pungent *largo viento* that suggests their painful, fruitless quest. Further lines of dialogue reinforce the effect. 'Where is your *niña amarga*?' (with an echo of the earlier *mar amarga*), the lover asks the father. The only reply is a recollection of how she was formerly, with fresh face and black hair, before the moon enveloped her in green and shade. The poem ends with the fullest restatement yet of the opening of the poem. But now the meaning is different. At the beginning the same four lines expressed a yearning for greenness and freshness and life. Now, at the end, new depths have been revealed. Green is not only the colour of freshness; it is also the colour of moon-induced (that is, fate-guided) putrefaction. One looks for life in its happiness and one finds life in its despair — like the girl, like her father, like her lover. The last four lines present a superposition of the two planes: on the one hand, life and longing; on the other, disillusion and death. Under life's happier appearances lies constantly, for Lorca, its inevitable tragedy: 'bajo la acacia en flor / del jardín, mi muerte acecha' (*Mariana Pineda*, II, 253).

Myth

This is one of the most important aspects of *Romancero gitano*. It is also the most widely emphasised and best studied.[3] Since the most helpful studies are easily available I can be brief. The book, said Lorca, begins with two invented myths: that of the moon as a dancer of death and that of the wind as a satyr (III, 342). The former will serve as an example. The moon comes down to the gypsy forge and carries away a child who is there alone. Emilio Castelar referred to the underlying superstition in a book published ten years before Lorca's birth — nurse-maids used to warn their young charges against looking too much at the moon 'pues recordábanse casos de haber bajado a comerse y tragarse los niños mirones' —[4] and Alvarez de Miranda has pointed to a more distant source in the death-bringing moon of primitive cultures (*15*, 41). Lorca, then, elaborated on an already existing myth. His invention lies in the way in which he incorporated the myth, as a mini-drama, into his gypsy world: 'mito de la luna sobre tierras de danza dramática', 'la luna como bailarina mortal' (III, 342), with emphasis on the oriental and ritualistic character of her dance, 'aquel "no descomponer pelo ni

---

[3] The poet himself referred to it in letters and lectures; his friend Melchor Fernández Almagro drew attention to it in a contemporary review (*5*) that Lorca saw as 'seguramente lo mejor que se ha hecho de mi libro' (III, 770); López-Morillas, in 1950, published an influential article on Lorca as a poet of myth (*12*), and in 1953 and 1957 Angel Alvarez de Miranda and Gustavo Correa respectively made this the central theme of two of the most revealing Lorca studies so far published: *La metáfora y el mito* in which the author sought to show how Lorca's poetry 'ha sido capaz de coincidir en todo lo esencial con los temas, motivos y mitos de antiguas religiones' (*15*, 12), and *La poesía mítica de FGL* in which six of Lorca's works were examined to illustrate the stylistic consequences of the poet's profoundly mythical vision (*21*). Innumerable other critics have since made their own contribution, often with widening of the concept of myth into Freudian and Jungian areas of depth psychology.

[4] *Galería histórica de mujeres célebres*, I, Madrid 1888, pp. 33–4.

rostro" de las grandes bailaoras, aquella serenidad de figura y majestad de cabeza y brazos'.[5] '¡Qué baile de amor y frío!', he wrote in an early draft of the poem (*A* I, 138). Love and seduction, but also icy detachment. The duality is developed throughout the dance. The bringing together of mythical moon and gypsy dancer is similarly significant and has general relevance. 'Desde los primeros versos se nota que el mito está mezclado con el elemento que pudiéramos llamar realista, aunque no lo es' (III, 342). The moon as a gypsy dancer is the apparently realistic element, the 'núcleo central' of the poem; the superstitions and fears associated with the traditional myth constitute the 'redonda perspectiva'. In his story of the gypsy moon's abduction of the child the poet creates an image with transcendental resonances; the reader, by his apprehension of the image, is brought into contact with the mystery of the transcendental. It is a duality that has been with us throughout the present study. Myth, it seems, is only an aspect of a far wider and more general feature of Lorca's style.

One could continue in similar fashion through the book and Correa especially has done so. Basically one can say of Lorca what he himself said of Góngora: 'transforma en mito cuanto toca' (III, 241). Sometimes, like Góngora, he alludes to classical myths, 'de una manera delicada y profunda, pero solamente comprensible a los que están en el secreto de la historia' (III, 241); at other times, again like Góngora (III, 240), he invents new myths. In 'Reyerta', for example, 'está expresada esa lucha sorda latente en Andalucía y en toda España de grupos que se atacan sin saber por qué, por causas misteriosas' (III, 343), a point that is echoed by the magistrate in the poem, with his ironic mythicising of the fight into an age-old conflict between Romans and Carthaginians (3:29–30). And in 'Romance de la Guardia Civil española', said Lorca, 'a veces, sin que se sepa por qué, [los guardias civiles] se convertirán en centuriones romanos' (III, 901), a view that was developed by Fernández Almagro in his 1928 review, with emphasis on the mythical aspect of the whole gypsy/civil guard conflict: 'Luchan la navaja y el mauser, como en el fondo mítico de todos los abolengos pelean dioses y titanes' (5, 374).

Romancero gitano, then, is a profoundly mythical work in which the here-and-now serves as a pointer to something far wider: mysterious

[5] Ricardo Molina, *Misterios del arte flamenco*, Barcelona 1967, p. 193. Molina is referring to Andalusian dancing in general, not to this poem.

and apparently uncontrollable forces, irrational fears and superstitions, power conflicts, primitive urges, a sense of human limitations, unfathomable questions of human destiny . . . . But certain poems are clearly more mythical than others and Lorca himself pointed especially to four: 'Romance de la luna, luna' and 'Preciosa y el aire' (in his lecture-reading), and these and two others in a note on the manuscript of 'San Gabriel': 'Romances miticos. Thamar. Preciosa. Luna luna. Olalla' (*A* I, 158). It is probable that at the time he wrote this note he did not intend including the 'Burla de Don Pedro' in *Romancero gitano* because of its formal anomalies.[6] But this poem too is notable for its mythical dimension. In short, the first two poems in the book and the last three. I make no further comment but consider their mythical character at length in my companion volume.

Nature's Involvement

I here take up a point that was made earlier in a brief reference to Lorca's use of natural settings. They are not mere settings, I suggested. Nature is alive and actively involved with the characters and their dilemmas. 'Thus, instead of a merely realistic background *monte* one finds a *monte oscuro* whose darkness complements the dark torment of character and action (7:3), and an *aire de poniente* appropriately accompanies Juan of Montilla's death (3:36) and *cielos quemados* are at one with Olalla's burnt body (16:68) and *nubes paradas* suggest shock and horror at Amnón's rape of his sister (18:84) and olives turn pale at the wind's pursuit of Preciosa (2:34) or await Antoñito's fateful night of Capricorn (11:21–2) . . .' (above, p. 17). It is something that one finds also in traditional *romances*, as in the following lines from the *Romancero del Cid*:

Considerad vuesas fijas	Tan hermosa iba Jimena,
amarradas a dos robles	que suspenso quedó el sol
de quien hoy tiemblan las hojas,	en medio de su carrera
condolidas de sus voces (*RC* 92).	por podella ver mejor (*RC* 23).

It is also something that Lorca associated both with *cante jondo*[7] and with the poetry of Góngora.[8] The effect is to broaden and enhance the

---

[6] Compare his reference to 'Romance de la luna, luna' as 'el primero que hice' (1926; III, 747), though it was surely composed after the 'Burla de Don Pedro' which exists in a manuscript dated 28 December 1921.

significance of what is presented, by transporting the reader, here too, from 'núcleo central' to 'redonda perspectiva'. We are touching on one of the most notable features of *Romancero gitano* and one that most clearly gives the work its characteristic epic and mythical quality.

In fact it is not only nature that responds to human actions and destiny. Objects too come alive in their involvement: the four lights of death, for example, that clamour in a gypsy wake (13:24–6), the relentless, *martinete*-like singing of hammers portending death (14:18–21), clocks that suddenly stop under the impact of the civil guards' onslaught, while fiery brandy disguises itself as cold November (15:77–80) . . . . Parts of the body too (3:25–6; 6:9–11, 32–3; 7:7–8 . . .). But above all, in every poem, elements of nature: a nightjar with its song of yearning (1:29–30), a wounded horse that beats at every door to warn of danger (15:29–30), the fig-tree that rubs its wind with the sandpaper of its branches, reminding us that the longed for *verde viento* and *verdes ramas* are both denied (4:17–18), the mountain that bristles up its bitter agaves under the threat of approaching danger (4:19–20), the stars that turn to bell-flowers — and little bells — in celebration of Saint Gabriel's glad tidings (10:37–8) and then to everlasting flowers, immortalised by the Annunciation (10:69–70) . . . . These all play a subordinate role compared with the moon in Poem 1 and the wind in Poem 2, but they serve similarly to broaden the impact of the action and to enhance its significance. One finds something similar in Lorca's metaphors, as in the much quoted and commented lines, *Los densos bueyes del agua / embisten a los muchachos / que se bañan en las lunas / de sus cuernos ondulados* (14:14–17). Moreover, these lines remind us that the surrounding world frequently comes alive not merely in passive response to human action but with indications of active and wilful initiative: *Las guitarras* suenan solas (10:19), *Fachadas de cal* ponían / *cuadrada y blanca la noche* (13:35–6), *Las piquetas de los*

---

[7] 'Todos los poemas del cante jondo son de un magnífico panteísmo, consulta al aire, a la tierra, al mar, a la luna, a cosas tan sencillas como el romero, la violeta y el pájaro. Todos los objetos exteriores toman una aguda personalidad y llegan a plasmarse hasta tomar parte activa en la acción lírica' (III, 209).

[8] 'Esta manera de animar y vivificar la Naturaleza es característica de Góngora. Necesita la conciencia de los elementos. Odia lo sordo y las fuerzas oscuras que no tienen límite [. . .]. Su sentimiento teogónico sublime da personalidad a las fuerzas de la Naturaleza' (III, 242).

gallos / cavan buscando *la aurora* (7:1–2), *Mil arbolillos de sangre* / [. . .] oponen *húmedos troncos* / *al bisturí de las llamas* (16:39–42), *Y el agua* se pone *fría* / para que *nadie la toque* (8:13–14), *la luna menguante* pone / *cabelleras amarillas* / *a las amarillas torres* (13:10–12), *la noche* busca *llanuras* / *porque* quiere *arrodillarse* (10:17–18), *La noche* se puso *íntima* / *como una pequeña plaza* (4:79–80). Here as elsewhere in *Romancero gitano* everything lives and throbs with vitality. One can refer, if one wishes, to personification. But it is difficult to imagine a context in which the word seems more anaemic and inadequate.

Two especially fine examples of nature's participation in the action of *Romancero gitano* were noted in earlier pages: 14:42–5, the pivotal lines of 'Romance del emplazado', between the foretelling of Amargo's death and its coming, where Saint James brandishes his cosmic sword as though approving the decree and the heavens turn their back in silence on the condemned man, and 18:1–12, in which nature, with its duality of detachment and involvement, anticipates the main theme of the poem. As a starting-point for further study the reader might use- fully consider the relevance of nature's response in a number of similar- ly impressive passages: 6:16–19; 11:17–24; 13:9–18 . . . . He will find many more.

NEO-PRIMITIVISM IN *ROMANCERO GITANO*

I have tried to show that Lorca elevates characters, actions and settings by a host of different but interacting means. The here-and-now per- sists, with all the immediacy and vividness that one associates with Lorca's poetry, but it takes on a higher significance too. It is akin to something that I have studied elsewhere in Lorca's writings under the name 'bisemic symbolism': on the one hand, a literal real plane; on the other, a symbolic evoked plane.[1] It is also akin to something that under the name 'disguised symbolism' has been studied as a basic charac- teristic of fifteenth-century painting: on the one hand, in line with the new Renaissance conquest of the visual world, an Annunciation or Nativity or Adoration scene that impresses by its domestic realism and immediacy of impact; on the other hand, in the same work and in line with the continuing tradition of medieval symbolism, a series of pointers

---

[1] Introduction to FGL, *La casa de Bernarda Alba*, Manchester 1983, xlvi ff.

to the higher significance of what is presented.[2] In Jan van Eyck, for example, 'all meaning has assumed the shape of reality; or, to put it the other way, all reality is saturated with meaning' (Panofsky, 144). The duality of the here-and-now and the transcendental in *Romancero gitano* can be expressed in similar terms and is similarly basic to Lorca's style. Nor is this the only similarity and three others at least are notable: ahistoricism, stylisation and the presence of visionary figures. Together these four characteristics constitute the basis of what I here refer to as Lorca's neo-primitivism. As a preliminary to what follows I emphasise that it is not a quest for sources. Like Devoto and Rizzo in their studies of the impact of traditional songs and ballads on Lorca's writings I seek to demonstrate stylistic affinity rather than specific influence. As Lorca was attracted by traditional songs and poems and found in them elements relevant to his own vision and art, so also, I suggest, with early painting.

First, the external evidence. As a student at the University of Granada, Lorca attended a course on theory of literature and the arts given by Professor Martín Domínguez Berrueta and participated in various study trips: to local monuments during 1915–16, especially the cathedral with its fine collection of fifteen-century paintings, principally Flemish;[3] further afield during 1916–17 on four excursions that were to be recalled in his teenage *Impresiones y paisajes* (1918).[4] In 1919 Lorca moved to Madrid where he would surely know the remarkable Flemish collection in the Prado, as well as Fra Angelico's charming *Annuncia-*

---

[2] Erwin Panofsky, *Early Netherlandish Painting* (Cambridge, Mass. 1966), I, 131–48 ('Reality and symbol in early Flemish painting'). See also Lloyd Benjamin, 'Disguised symbolism exposed and the history of early Netherlandish painting', in *Studies in Iconography* 2 (1976), 11–24.

[3] 'Berrueta conocía muy bien la colección de cuadros primitivos de la Capilla Real [. . .] y Gómez Ortega [a fellow student of Lorca] recordaba las muchas horas que pasaron él, Lorca y Mariscal allí con el maestro, embebidos en la contemplación de las magníficas obras de Memling y Van der Weyden, y de *La oración del Huerto* de Botticelli' (Gibson, I, *FGL*, 110).

[4] Gibson, I, 114–15. As the visit to Covarrubias shows, Lorca disguised neither his scorn nor his enthusiasm: scorn, for example, for the popularly revered statues of St Cosmas and St Damian ('dos muñecos de caras estúpidas vestidos de un damasco descolorido'); enthusiasm for 'el gran retablo flamenco de la Adoración de los Magos' and 'algún interior flamenco que tiene la luz admirable de Vermeer' (III, 38–9).

tion. And of course he travelled and, as Baedeker noted in 1913, 'Those who pass from town to town in almost any Spanish province will receive the impression that in the 15th cent. every church possessed one or more painted retablos, so great is the number that have been preserved' (*Spain and Portugal*, 4th ed., lxxv).

Lorca, then, was familiar with early painting and, as my footnote quotations show, he was enthusiastic about it. He also had ample opportunity both to develop familiarity and to indulge enthusiasm, and as a painter himself he doubtless did both. Rafael Alberti strengthens this supposition with evidence of Lorca's delight in primitive imagery. He is recalling their first meeting (1924), when Alberti himself was still known principally as a painter:

> Me dijo, entre otras cosas, haber visto, años atrás, mi exposición del Ateneo; que yo era su primo y que deseaba encargarme un cuadro en el que se le viera dormido a orillas de un arroyo y arriba, allá en lo alto de un olivo, la imagen de la Virgen, ondeando en una cinta la siguiente leyenda: "Aparición de Nuestra Señora del Amor Hermoso al poeta Federico García Lorca" (*La arboleda perdida*, Buenos Aires 1959, p. 172).

One notes two things especially: the image of the Virgin 'en lo alto de un olivo' and the worded scroll. Both suggest early painting and the former is echoed in *Romancero gitano*:

> En la copa de un olivo
> lloran dos viejas mujeres (3:9–10).[5]

Similarly, in the closing paragraph of his lecture on Góngora's poetic imagery Lorca evoked the Cordoban poet's death: 'Poco después, su alma, dibujada y bellísima como un arcángel de Mantegna, calzadas

---

[5] Compare also the following, from a traditional *romance*:

> En una rama más alta,
> viera estar una infantina;
> cabellos de su cabeza
> todo el roble cobrían (*RVC* 151).

Stylistic similarities between early painting and contemporary early *romances* abound. It is the point at which the influence of the traditional *romance* (above, 'The *romance* tradition') and the influence of early painting come together and are seen as related aspects of Lorca's neo-primitivism in *Romancero gitano*. The subject merits further study.

sandalias de oro, al aire su túnica amaranto, sale a la calle en busca de
la escala vertical que subirá serenamente' (III, 247). Here too the neo-
primitive note is unmistakable, with a reference to Jacob's ladder,
widely represented in Christian art and 'regarded as a "type" of the
Virgin Mary, through whom a union of heaven and earth was accom-
plished'.[6] And like the figure in the olive tree this image too is relevant
to *Romancero gitano*, for it anticipates Saint Gabriel's leave-taking,
significantly from a gypsy virgin: *Ya San Gabriel en el aire / por una
escala subía* (10:67–8). But Lorca's evocation of Góngora's death
illustrates a further point, for there appears to be no such painting of an
archangel by Mantegna. As with traditional *romances*, then, it is not a
question of mere calque or imitation. With paintings as with *romances*
Lorca interiorised and developed what he found. It is something that
we observe throughout *Romancero gitano*: in a poem like 'San Gabriel'
where characters and theme clearly echo early painting, in poems like
the 'Martirio de Santa Olalla' where, somewhat less obviously, there
are thematic and iconographical resonances of a much painted subject,
the Crucifixion, and in poems like 'Romance de la luna, luna' where
there is no thematic or iconographic resemblance. In *Romancero
gitano* more than elsewhere, it seems, Lorca's own vision and style
found support in the vision and style of early Renaissance artists. To
demonstrate both specific similarities and the wider relevance of those
similarities I shall start, under each of the headings that follow, with
evidence from 'San Gabriel', where the parallel to early painting is
most striking, and thereafter broaden the range to show how Lorca's
neo-primitivism extends to areas where there is no immediate parallel.
To obviate extensive quotation from critical works on painting, I must
assume that the reader unfamiliar with the subject will look at relevant
illustrations in a history of art or, more ambitiously, consult both plates
and commentary in a standard work such as Erwin Panofsky's *Early
Netherlandish Painting* or Gertrud Schiller's *Iconography of Christian
Art* (trans. J. Seligman, 2 vols., London 1971–72).

Immediacy and Significance

On the one hand, immediacy, 'núcleo central'; on the other, signi-
ficance, 'redonda perspectiva'. It has been the main theme of my study

[6] J. Hall, *Dictionary of Subjects and Symbols in Art*, London 1974,
p. 164.

and I can here be brief. 'San Gabriel (Sevilla)', for example, like count-less fifteenth-century Annunciations, is notable for its domestic inti-macy and immediacy of impact. But we are struck also by the poem's refined elevation of tone and its wider resonances. Saint Gabriel appears as a local gypsy boy but he is also the biblical archangel and a Sevillian *par excellence* and he receives appropriate cosmic homage. Similarly, Anunciación, a gypsy girl, with delightfully Sevillian turns of speech, is also the local patron saint (and thence the biblical Annunciate) and an archetypal *linda gitana*. The lines *abre la puerta al lucero / que por la calle venía* illustrate the duality further, with a nice mingling of domestic realism and cosmic symbol. In all this the poem is notably neo-primitive and comparable dualities have been observed in studies on early paintings of the Annunciation.

One finds something similar in the 'Martirio de Santa Olalla'. Here we are told little about the protagonist herself, but we know that Lorca originally saw her as a gypsy girl and the juxtaposition of gypsy and saint ('la gitana Santa Olalla', III, 901) was apparently a means of elevating the gypsy by association, in the same way that Anunciación is elevated. For the rest, Lorca's emphasis is on the horror of martyrdom and its impact on the world around. The former, we shall see, is glori-fied by echoes of the Passion of Christ; the latter by evidence of nature's rebirth. The here-and-now of torture and killing, then, is elevated by biblical and iconographic resonances and goes hand in hand with pointers to resurrection and new life that reach their climax in the closing lines of the poem, with cosmic monstrance, apotheosis and mass. This is wholly in line with early Renaissance painting. So is the tripartite division of the poem, with its reminder of an altar triptych.

In the Antoñito poems we move away from any immediately obvious thematic similarity to religious painting. The interplay of the here-and-now and the transcendental, however, persists, prompted by a series of techniques that serve to elevate and magnify both Antoñito and his misfortunes: the subtle exploitation of Spanish language and *romance* form, the echoing of *cante* and *romances*, references to local culture and traditions (including the Holy Week processions), biblical reson-ances, traditional Christian iconography, pointers to nature's involve-ment, echoes of Greek tragedy. The techniques are for the most part different from those of the fifteenth-century painter. The resulting duality, however, is basically the same: individual immediacy and cosmic dimension. The ministering angels at the end of the poem are there to emphasise the point.

As a final example of the interplay of the here-and-now and the transcendental I recall my earlier comments on a poem in which I find no religious resonances: 'Romance de la pena negra'. It is one of the finest poems in the book and the one that most closely captures the dark passion and fatalism of Andalusian *cante jondo*. The night of Soledad Montoya, said Lorca, is a 'concreción de la Pena sin remedio, de la pena negra de la cual no se puede salir más que abriendo con un cuchillo un ojal bien hondo en el costado siniestro' (III, 343–4). The physical darkness of the opening lines, then, is an image of the emotive *pena negra* of the title and Soledad Montoya, associated by name with both the dark mountain (*monte/Montoya*) and the darkness of her own solitude (*Soledad*), is involved, like the *gallos* in the opening line, in a quest for light. But her quest is not merely individual and anecdotic. 'La Pena de Soledad Montoya es la raíz del pueblo andaluz' (III, 344). In the final lines of the poem the parallel between the search of the roosters and the search of the gypsies as represented by Soledad Montoya is broken: the cocks have found their dawn; Soledad Montoya and the gypsies have not. The delight of the dawn urges upon us, by contrast, the persistence (with hidden course and far-off dawn) of the gypsies' own black sorrow. Again, then, the individual (both character and setting) has wider resonances. The same duality again as in early painting. But not only in painting. Rafael Cansinos Assens, a notable authority on Andalusian *cante jondo*, writes: 'En la copla andaluza solloza como en un vasto Miserere todo el dolor irredimible de un pueblo, todo el dolor irredimible de la humanidad, aunque expresado con los acentos de un duelo personal e íntimo'.[7] There is no reference to Lorca, much less to fifteenth-century painting. But the relevance of his observation is striking: on the one hand, 'un duelo personal e íntimo' (the individual here-and-now); on the other, all the irredeemable grief of a people, of humanity itself (the wider significance). As in Lorca and as in early painting, 'all reality is saturated with meaning' (Panofsky). Only in one respect might one suspect a difference: in early painting the higher meaning relates to an accepted system of values existing outside the work of art; in Lorca and *cante*, as in the best ballad literature, this is not so; resonances are uncontoured; 'La escala llega a la luna.'

---

[7] *La copla andaluza* [1933], Madrid 1976, p. 29.

Ahistoricism

In the title 'San Gabriel (Sevilla)' a biblical saint of the past and an Andalusian city of the present are juxtaposed. The juxtaposition epitomises the second neo-primitive feature of the poem: its lack of historical perspective. As Fra Angelico depicted his Annunciations in a wholly fifteenth-century Italian context (dress, hairstyle, book of hours, Brunelleschi-style loggia) and as the Master of Flémalle and Rogier van der Weyden depicted theirs in a fifteenth-century Flemish context, so Lorca, as an ostensibly gypsy narrator, presents his own Annunciation in local and contemporary gypsy terms. Characters, description, imagery, echoes of *cante*, speech — all contribute to the effect and, like the domestic intimacy of early painting, serve to bring the scene close to us, in contrast to sixteenth- and seventeenth-century Annunciations with their often forbidding monumentality and, in so far as Annunciations continued to be painted, in contrast also to the spectator-distancing historical perspectivism of the eighteenth and nineteenth centuries. With his own Annunciation Lorca overleaps four centuries of European artistic tradition and returns to a wholly primitive — that is, wholly contemporary — vision of the Annunciation. Until the twentieth-century advent of neo-primitivism it is something that one associates less with Europe's post-Raphaelite artistic traditions than with the art of less historically-minded communities of the present: Africans who transpose biblical stories into an African context, Amerindians who transpose them into an American context, gypsies who transpose them into a gypsy context.[8] It is this that Lorca, in his assumed role as gypsy narrator, does in 'San Gabriel'.

But he creates his own stories too and treats them in similar neo-primitive fashion. In 'Romance de la Guardia Civil española' the Virgin and Saint Joseph have lost their castanets and search out the gypsies for help in finding them (15:37–40). The anachronism is akin to that of early paintings in which medieval saints, doctors of the Church and the donors of the painting appear as worshippers in a Nativity or Adoration or representation of Madonna and Child. But Lorca, now, is drawing not so much on painting as on a nativity scene of the type

---

[8] On the last point see Juan de Dios Ramírez-Heredia, *Nosotros los gitanos*, Barcelona 1972; second and third photographs between pp. 96 and 97.

that Spanish children prepare each Christmas: the Virgin attired with all the splendour of a mayor's wife, in silver paper, with a necklace of almonds, and Saint Joseph in a silk cape. And what more natural, for the Andalusian gypsy, especially since we are in Jerez de la Frontera, than that the three wise men should be accompanied by the king of sherry? In the onslaught that follows, the gypsies, noted for their veneration of the parents of Christ, are naturally assisted by Saint Joseph and the Virgin and, in the doorway of Bethlehem (with echoes of *belén* as *crèche*, *Nativity tableau*; a reminder of lines 41–8), Saint Joseph shrouds a dead girl and the Virgin, with a gypsy-like cure elevated to cosmic level, tends the wounded children. In November 1926, while he was working on the poem, Lorca wrote to Guillén: 'Las escenas del saqueo serán preciosas. A veces, sin que se sepa por qué, [los guardias civiles] se convertirán en centuriones romanos' (III, 901). This idea was subsequently abandoned, it seems, but the comment is revealing. Persecutors and oppressors exist in all ages. So do their victims. The historicist will be inclined to see them in their respective historical contexts and thus to distinguish between them. For Lorca, with a less historicist view and a powerful emotive response to the horror of oppression and the suffering of its victims, the oppressors and victims of one period in history are easily fused with the oppressors and victims of another period. The 'Romance del emplazado', clearly based on the fate of Ferdinand IV 'el Emplazado' but applied by Lorca to a gypsy, is part of the same phenomenon. So is the anachronistic inclusion of the 'tres romances históricos' in an alleged gypsy ballad-book. Even the dismissive comment of the magistrate in 'Reyerta' on the death of a gypsy, *Han muerto cuatro romanos / y cinco cartagineses* (3:29–30), suggests a similar awareness of time's obsessive repetition.

   I pass now to a more specific example of Lorca's ahistoricism and again start with 'San Gabriel'. The number three appears three times in the poem: first the *tres clavos de alegría* that pierce Anunciación (40), then the *tres heridas* foretold for the child (54), finally the *tres balas de almendra verde* that tremble in the child's voice and suggest that prophecy is already being fulfilled (65). Though not mentioned in the Gospels, nails appear frequently — always three of them — in fifteenth-century Descents from the Cross, Pietàs and Arma Christi and there are examples of all these in the Granada collection that Lorca enthused over as a student.[9] The three nails, then, are a symbolic pointer to the

---

[9] On the history of the three nails (reduced from the four of earlier

Crucifixion and it is as such that they appear in Lorca's poem, with progression from three nails of joy to three wounds foretold and on to three bullets of bitter almond in the unborn child's voice. Even amidst the joy of the Annunciation, he suggests, the horror of death threatens. It is basic to Lorca's fatalistic vision. It is also an example of a device that Carlos Bousoño has identified and studied under the name 'superposición temporal': the simultaneous presentation of different and usually emotively contrasted moments in time. For Bousoño it is exclusive to the twentieth century and reveals the poet's obsession with time's passing (which Bousoño associates with historicism).[10] 'Del eternismo inmovilista de la Edad Media,' he comments, 'hemos pasado al dinamismo aceleradamente temporalista de nuestra edad Contemporánea' (391). But the fifteenth century, for example, was notably aware of time's passing (François Villon, Jorge Manrique, dances of death . . .) and revealed its awareness in an almost obsessive emphasis on *ubi sunt* themes. Besides, Bousoño is surely wrong to invoke historicism as an explanation. Historicism involves a particular response to the consciousness of time's passing, with an excessively rational and somewhat outdated emphasis on historical determinism and the diachronic concatenation of events, something that we now associate especially with the eighteenth and nineteenth centuries. Conceivably it is not historicism that explains temporal superposition as a modern phenomenon but, on the contrary, the breakdown of confidence in the over-rational historicist perception of time. If this is true we should expect to find examples of temporal superposition in earlier, less rigidly rational periods of European culture. In painting at least they abound, and 'San Gabriel' — like Bousoño's own 'Cristo adolescente', with its superposition of the Cross of the Crucifixion on Christ's childhood — has distinguished forebears, especially in the fifteenth and sixteenth centuries, with the frequent incorporation of pointers to Christ's death into Annunciations, Nativities, Adorations and representations of the Madonna and Child. Indeed, it is one of the most notable stylistic features of early Renaissance religious painting, completely at one with the *tres balas de almendra verde* that tremble in the

Christian art) see Schiller, II, esp. 137–46; also Thematic index, 'Nails', and dozens of illustrations). By the mid-thirteenth century 'the three nails play a large part in devotions relating to the Passion, for they are among the most important of the *Arma Christi*' (II, 146).

[10] *Teoría de la expresión poética*. 6th ed., Madrid 1976, I, 389–411.

unborn child's voice as Lorca's Saint Gabriel takes his leave.[11] But again there is no question of a coldly intellectual calque on fifteenth-century style. Like the interplay of the here-and-now and the transcendental the perception of death in life is basic to Lorca's own vision. Temporal superposition can reasonably be seen as an expression of this. '¿Qué sientes en tu boca / roja y sedienta?' children ask the poet in one of his earliest poems. 'El sabor de los huesos/de mi gran calavera,' he replies (I.97). 'Bajo la acacia en flor / del jardín,' says Mariana Pineda, 'mi muerte acecha' (II, 253). In 'Nacimiento de Cristo' (*Poeta en Nueva York*) Lorca returns to the obsessive three nails of the Crucifixion:

> El niño llora y mira con un tres en la frente.
> San José ve en el heno tres espinas de bronce (I, 484).

[11] I offer examples from only a few especially famous works: in the Master of Flémalle's Annunciation in the Mérode altarpiece (*c.* 1425) the tiny figure of the Infant Christ who descends in the rays of the Holy Spirit bears a cross (cf. Schiller, I, Figs. 101–4, for four similar examples); in Hugo van der Goes's Berlin Nativity (before 1482) the shape of the manager significantly resembles a sarcophagus (cf. B. G. Lane, *The Altar and the Altarpiece*, New York 1984, p. 57, for commentary on the frequency of this); in the Adoration of the Magi in Rogier van der Weyden's Columba Altarpiece the manger again resembles a sarcophagus and a crucifix hangs on the pillar behind the Virgin and Child; in the central panel of Hieronymus Bosch's Epiphany triptych in the Prado (1495) the first king's gift, a statuette of the sacrifice of Isaac, 'prefigures Christ's coming sacrifice' (Lane, p. 66); in the Isenheim altar (*c.* 1515) the Christ child's clothes, in the Nativity, have holes in them that anticipate the holed loin-cloth of the Crucifixion . . . To these and many more can be added also countless paintings in which the Christ child holds a goldfinch, a further pointer to the Passion since, according to legend, the goldfinch 'acquired its red spot at the moment when it flew down over the head of Christ on the road to Calvary and, as it drew a thorn from his brow, was splashed with a drop of the Saviour's blood' (Hall, 330–1). I am assured that in poetry similar temporal superposition continued into the seventeenth century, as in the following lines from a 'Romance de Natividad' by Valdivielso (*Romancero espiritual*, ed. 1648):

> Este cayado le traigo [al zagal recién nacido],
> hecho cruz, porque imagino
> que se ha de quedar crabado
> por guardar su ganadillo.

Lest we still have doubts about the relevance of such superposition to Lorca's own emotive response to the world around, the following lines, from a letter by the poet to Sebastián Gasch, make it clear: 'Me conmueve; me produce Dalí la misma emoción pura (y que Dios Nuestro Señor me perdone) que me produce el niño Jesús abandonado en el Pórtico de Belén, con todo el germen de la crucifixión ya latente bajo las pajas de la cuna' (1927; III, 968). In art as in real life, it seems, Lorca's vision was the same. It was affinity rather than a mere desire to imitate that drew him to the fifteenth century. The lack of historical perspective noted in 'San Gabriel' offers further evidence, for, like temporal superposition, it presupposes rejection of the historicist's rigidly linear and determinist notion of temporal progression and thereby brings Lorca close to the ahistoricism of an earlier age. The muting of narrative progression in his poems and the enhanced dependence on 'tensión lírica' resulting from the interplay of 'redondas perspectivas' is arguably part of the same phenomenon.[12]

In a recent article Derek Harris has pointed to some of Lorca's many references to the Crucifixion (53). He is perhaps most perceptive on 'Muerto de amor' where he finds echoes of the death of Christ. The following lines complement and reinforce his findings:

> Brisas de caña mojada
> y rumor de viejas voces
> resonaban por el arco
> roto de la media noche.
> Bueyes y rosas dormían (13:19–23).

In context the last line suggests innocent unawareness of the surrounding violence of death and suffering. But as countless early paintings demonstrate, oxen are also much associated with the stable at Bethlehem. Nor is it only the oxen. The immediately preceding *arco roto* recalls one of the most frequent images of ruin in early Nativities and Adorations (Lane, 65) and Lorca had easy access to an example in the Prado: Hans Memling's Adoration, which has both ox and broken arches. As for the roses, traditional iconography again offers the essential clue, for the rose is associated with the Virgin Mary and Lorca himself made the connection in a little-known poem: 'Rosas, rosas, joyas vivas de

---

[12] Ramsden, 'Round perspective and lyric tension in *Romancero gitano*', in *'Cuando yo me muera ...': Essays in Memory of Federico García Lorca*, ed. C. B. Morris, University Press of America [at press].

infinito [...] / tenéis en vuestro ser / una esencia divina: / María de Nazaret' (I, 989–90).[13] The case seems sure. Amidst echoes of the death of Christ there is also a tacit reminder of His birth. It is another example of temporal superposition. But whereas in 'San Gabriel' the real plane was the birth and the evoked plane the death (that is, with the superposition of future time on present time), in 'Muerto de amor' the real plane is the death and the evoked plane the birth (with the superposition of past time on present time). Fifteenth-century examples of the former abound but, except for the occasional presence of the Annunciation lily in paintings of the Christ of Sorrows, Lamentations and Last Judgments, I know of no examples of the latter and it is probable that Lorca too was unaware of any. In 'Muerto de amor', it seems, the poet did not simply follow a primitive stylistic device; in line with his own ahistoricism and sensitivity to time's passing he here developed the device to bring out the horror and injustice and pathos of the death. In an earlier section I pointed to comparable examples of Lorca's development of *romance* techniques beyond anything found in traditional *romances*. His evocation of an apparently fictitious painting by Mantegna is part of the same creative phenomenon. With paintings as with *romances*, I repeat, Lorca interiorised and developed what he found. It is something that we observe throughout *Romancero gitano*.

Stylisation

In September 1923 Lorca wrote to Fernández Almagro of his aims in *Mariana Pineda*:

> Yo quiero hacer un drama *procesional* ..., una narración *simple* e *hierática*, rodeada de evocaciones y brisas misteriosas, como una vieja madonna con su arco de querubines.
>
> Una especie de cartelón de ciego *estilizado*. Un crimen, en suma, donde el rojo de la sangre se confunda con el rojo de las cortinas (III, 727).

Two points are relevant to the present section: his desire for stylisation (a point that he makes also about other works; about *Poema del cante jondo*, for example, which he described as 'estilizadamente popular',

---

[13] Cf. 'Rose. A flower particularly association with the Virgin Mary who is called the "rose without thorns", i.e. sinless' (Hall, 268).

III, 778)[14] and his association of this with neo-primitive imagery ('una vieja madonna con su arco de querubines'). It is in *Romancero gitano* where these two things most clearly come together and give the work its distinctive character. What started with a progression from the here-and-now world of the senses to a realm of mystery and uncontoured forces here takes on sensuous form again on a stylised plane of metaphor and symbol. It is one of the keys to Lorca's anti-Romanticism.

Stylisation in 'San Gabriel' reveals itself in two ways: by the use of traditional iconography, as in early religious painting (doves, bells, stars, flowers — especially the white Annunciation lily —, nails, ladder), and by the presence of tonally similar elements of the poet's own invention (*piel de nocturna manzana, plata caliente, dalias del aire, pecho de jaspe* . . .). There is a similar duality in the 'Martirio de Santa Olalla': on the one hand, traditional Christian iconography (dicing soldiers, sleeping figures insensitive to nearby agony, crowing cock, crown of thorns, lance in the side, severed breasts and hands, angels and seraphims); on the other, similarly stylised imagery (*caballo de larga cola, medio monte de Minervas, agua en vilo, quiebra el cristal de las copas, un chorro de venas verdes* . . .). Lorca, it seems, moves easily between direct indebtedness and mere similarity. My inference, as in previous sections, is that there is an underlying affinity of vision and technique.

I pass over much comparable stylisation — individual images (*un sillón de clavellinas*, 10:50; *rosas de pólvora negra*, 15:112 . . .), the stylising use of the diminutive (*domador de palomillas*, 10:21; *salivilla de estrella*, 15:100 . . .), the incorporation of archangels and their associated symbols (lily, fish, orb) . . . — and concentrate on a single area common to early religious painting and to *Romancero gitano*: that of wound imagery. As a starting-point one may recall the symbolic three nails of the Crucifixion referred to earlier and their various echoes in 'San Gabriel'. Immediately comparable are the *cinco llagas de Cristo* of 'La monja gitana' (5:19), much represented in fifteenth-century paint-

---

[14] See also his approval of stylisation in the work of others: of Góngora the poet ('Hesíodo cuenta su *Teogonía* con fervor popular y religioso, y el sutil cordobés la vuelve a contar estilizada o inventando nuevos mitos', III, 240) and of Dalí the painter ('Estilizas o copias después de haber mirado', I, 955). One may recall also his enthusiasm for *cante jondo*: 'No hay nada, absolutamente nada, igual en toda España, ni en estilización, ni en ambiente, ni en justeza emocional' (III, 205).

ing.[15] Next, *manos cortadas*. They appear twice in *Romancero gitano* (13:47, 16:32), as well as in a drawing by Lorca (III, 1041), and they too are frequent in early paintings, both in martyrdoms and in numerous Arma Christi (twelve examples in Schiller, II, Figs. 661–774). Similarly, *Rosa la de los Camborios* and Olalla are both described with their severed breasts placed on a tray (15:107–8; 16:25–6, 45–50), a reminder of paintings of the martyred Saint Agatha, commonly depicted carrying her breasts on a tray. We are reminded too, by the common fate of contemporary gypsy girl (Rosa) and early Christian martyr (Olalla), of a point made earlier about Lorca's ahistoricism: that differences in time fade for him before the repeated sameness of horror. I continue with wound imagery. *Trescientas rosas morenas* (4:41), as an image of a gypsy smuggler's wounds, is clearly stylised and equally clearly in harmony with the imagery of early Christian art where one does, on occasion, find blood that turns to flowers.[16] But similar stylisation is found also in present-day Andalusian Holy Week tableaux where red roses are used to represent the blood that flows from the Virgin Mary's pierced heart. Lorca may conceivably have been influenced by one or the other, or by neither. Here as elsewhere, it is not the presence or absence of a given source that matters in *Romancero gitano* but the author's neo-primitive stylising vision. There is a similar range of possibilities in *su cuerpo lleno de lirios / y una granada en las sienes* (3:19–20). In the image of *lirios* as wounds one notes that 'the iris with its sword-shaped leaves is a recurring symbol of the Passion of Christ' (Schiller, I, 51); in the image of the *granada*, on the other hand, one recalls, perhaps more relevantly, that in Andalusian usage a *granada* commonly indicates a contused wound. Direct influence or creative affinity? In my last examples at least the stylisation, it seems, is wholly personal: *Mis hilos de sangre tejen / volantes sobre tu falda* (18: 59–60) and *Corales tibios dibujan / arroyos en rubio mapa* (18:75–6). As in the previous paragraph, we have passed from evidence of direct indebtedness to traditional imagery to mere stylistic similarity. The distinction, of course, is artificial. Lorca passes easily between one and

---

[15] 'The main consequence of [St Francis of Assisi's] stygmatization was veneration of Christ's five wounds, which became very common during the fifteenth century' (Schiller, II, 190; five examples in Figs. 668–73).

[16] Schiller has noted a fourteenth-century Arma Christi in which an appended contemporary note states explicitly that the five bleeding roses on the Cross symbolise Christ's wounds (II, 192; Fig. 655).

the other, integrating both traditional image and personal invention into his own uniquely stylised gypsy ballads. Anyone familiar with early paintings of martyrdoms will recognise the similar duality of impact: vivid immediacy and emotional detachment. In contrast to the Romantics with their soft-centred imagery and their clamour for the reader's personal involvement, Lorca invites his reader to a vividly evoked 'baile de amor y frío' (*A* I, 138), 'un crimen donde el rojo de la sangre se confunda con el rojo de las cortinas' (III, 727). An emotive response but with detachment. It is basic to his art. It is also relevant to his enthusiasm for the puppet theatre.

In the above I have suggested the influence of traditional Christian iconography. But there are similarities also to secular painting. As an example I invite the reader to look at 'Reyerta', lines 9–22. It is one of the most stylised and painting-influenced passages in *Romancero gitano* and except for lines 11–12 all the images have been commented on in previous pages or will be commented on in the following section. Lines 11–12 alone seem to have no neo-primitive resonances. In them the poet gives physical form to a popular expression (*subirse por las paredes, to go off the deep end, climb up the wall*) and shows a mythical bull of strife (the epitome of animal power) as he actually clambers up walls (like a bull climbing up the *barrera* of a bullring). But this is exactly the sort of thing that Bruegel did in the sixteenth century in painting, with his literal representation of expressions such as *armed to the teeth, falling beween two stools, running one's head against a brick wall, speaking with two mouths* and a hundred or so more.[17] I find it difficult to accept that Lorca, both as an art student and as an enthusiast of painting, was not aware of this. Without this assumption lines 11–12 stand strangely apart from the profuse painterly references of the rest of the passage.

I conclude with a brief reference to lines from Lorca's opening description of Merida in the 'Martirio de Santa Olalla': *Medio monte de Minervas / abre sus brazos sin hojas* (16:5–6). As in 'Preciosa y el aire' where a gypsy girl comes along playing her tambourine *por un anfibio sendero / de cristales y laureles* (2:3–4), to be pursued shortly by the big-man wind, I find an echo of a classical subject much represented in early Renaissance painting: Daphne's flight from Apollo and her transformation into a laurel tree. Of the dozen or so paintings of the subject

---

[17] On this and the pre-Bruegel tradition of such painting see Walter S. Gibson, *Bruegel*, London 1977, pp. 65–79.

known to me those most evoked by Lorca's lines show Daphne in flight, her arms uplifted, with leaves sprouting where her fingers had been (cf. also Bernini's seventeenth-century statue of the same subject in the Villa Borghese, Rome). In his evocation of the comatose and mutilated civilisation of Rome, Lorca presents a panorama of mutilated statues with no leaves sprouting where the hands had been. Since Minerva was both the goddess of war and one of the great triad of state divinities, the image of lost martial and civic vitality is impressive. It is Olalla's martyrdom, Lorca will suggest, that brings the awaited rebirth.

Visionary Figures

I am far from exhausting the subject of iconographic resonances and stylisation in *Romancero gitano* and one aspect merits separate treatment. I refer to the angels and other visionary figures who appear in the work: Saint Gabriel, for example, who, having completed his mission, ascends a ladder to heaven amidst stars eternalised by the Annunciation (10:67–70); seraphims who play accordions (13:37–8); angels who minister to the dead Antoñito (12:45–8) .... In the context of *Romancero gitano*, under the joint impact of biblical resonances, Christian iconography and traditions of the Andalusian Holy Week, one should perhaps find no problem here, any more than one should at the presence of the Virgin and Saint Joseph in a gypsy town under attack by the Civil Guard. To the present writer at least they are wholly visionary figures, part of Christian tradition and of the gypsies' world of magic. But this is not the usual interpretation. Mena, for example, notes 'la eliminación de hechos irreales o maravillosos' in traditional *romances* and seeks to apply this also to *Romancero gitano*: 'Aunque es verdad que en el *Romancero gitano*, de Lorca, parece encontrarse un mundo irreal y fantástico, esto es debido más bien al uso de sus metáforas, y no a que describa situaciones o personajes irreales' (*42*, 29). I find myself unable to accept this. Nor am I wholly convinced by Correa's repeated attempts to demystify Lorca's angels. On lines 45–8 of 'Muerte de Antoñito el Camborio', for example, he comments as follows: 'La presencia del amanecer se hace luego más evidente y el cielo con la presencia de los ángeles (nubes) colabora en un rito funerario dando almohada al muerto y encendiendo un *candil* funerario (el sol rojizo y opaco en el cielo marchoso)' (*21*, 41). Characteristically Correa breaks down the image of the angels and their actions into constituent parts and offers a real-life (bracketed) explanation of each in terms of natural phenomena. He may be justified in doing so but I do not feel that he is. Nor am I convinced that there is here any indication of daybreak. Besides, if a natural explanation is offered for *candil* it seems fair to ask for a corresponding explanation of *cojín*, which Correa does not give. Fragmentary, real-life explanation, I suggest, is inappropriate to Lorca's visionary world. The poet's own observation on 'Romance sonámbulo', lines 59–60, seems relevant: 'Si me preguntan ustedes por qué digo yo: "Mil panderos de cristal herían la madrugada", les diré que los he visto en manos de ángeles' (III, 343) — a clear affirmation of his own magical, non-analytical vision. In the context of the Antoñito poems it is almost self-evident that angels will attend the hero at his death and that, in ministering to him, they will follow time-honoured tradition and place a cushion (not a pillow) beneath his head and light an oil-lamp for the vigil. Clouds and the allegedly dawning sky, I suggest, have nothing to do with it. We are touching on an aspect of Lorcan interpretation — and of critical disagreement — on which the reader eventually has to take his stand.

There are similar examples in 'Reyerta'. A fight between gypsies takes on epic dimensions and is appropriately attended by black angels:

> Angeles negros traían
> pañuelos y agua de nieve.
> Angeles con grandes alas
> de navajas de Albacete (3:13–16).

At the end of the poem, when the fight is over, they take their leave:

> Y ángeles negros volaban
> por el cielo de poniente.
> Angeles de largas trenzas
> y corazones de aceite (3:35–8).

Again 'natural' explanations are usual: 'Those who are succouring the distressed need not necessarily refer to supernatural angels, but gypsy women, and their "wings" would be the long shadows of their shawls on the late afternoon hillside' (Campbell, 44); 'Los nubarrones se van perfilando como ángeles negros con sus grandes alas relucientes, largas trenzas y negros corazones' (Correa, 28); 'Failing light finds the wounded thighs of the horsemen while black angels — the last of evening clouds — keep vigil' (Loughran);[18] 'unas nubes amenazadoras de

---

[18] In *The World of Nature in the Works of FGL*, ed. J. W. Zdenek, Rock Hill, South Carolina: Winthrop Studies, 1980, p. 57.

lluvia personificadas en ángeles que traen pañuelos y agua pura'
(López Castellón, 11). Such explanations may be justified, but the
combination of epic dimension, stylisation and overall context does not
convince me that they are, any more than I find it justified to invoke
clouds to explain the many angels who fly around fifteenth-century
Crucifixions — including the black angels (figures and clothes) in
Memling's famous Vienna triptych or the angels in Dierick Bouts's
Rogier-influenced Crucifixion in Granada Cathedral. Besides, if one
offers a natural explanation for the *ángeles negros*, one must surely do
the same for the superb image of Juan Antonio as he rides his cross of
fire along the highway to death (21–2). But Campbell and Correa omit
reference to it, López Castellón says simply that Juan Antonio has
changed his horse for a cross of fire and Loughran, who is alone con-
sistent, offers another natural explanation, finding 'a direct allusion to
the setting sun, the daily victim of a cosmic vendetta that is as "real"
and predictable as the clash of passions among men' (*loc. cit.*). If one
accepts my view of Lorca's neo-primitivism there is no need to explain
the image at all. It is wholly consistent with his magical vision that a
gypsy horseman and hero should make his exit from the world mounted
on a cross of fire.

My final example of Lorca's use of angels is from the 'Martirio de
Santa Olalla':

> Angeles y serafines
> dicen: Santo, Santo, Santo (16:73–4).

The angels here are completely in harmony with other angels in
Romancero gitano and it would seem logical that critics who explain
those other angels by reference to natural phenomena should do the
same with these. To the best of my knowledge none has done so.
Understandably, for this line is a direct quotation from Catholic
liturgy. The angels here are certainly supernatural, visionary figures.

Having considered a number of examples where my suggestion of
visionary figures is supported by traditional Christian iconography I
turn finally to a figure for whom I can claim no such direct support. I
refer to the moon in the opening poem of the book. It has prompted
more natural explanations than any other figure. McInnes and Bohning,
who carrying naturalism further than most, comment as follows:

> The particular features of the moon's personification are derived
> from the effect of full moonlight falling on the forge and the anvil.

Her starched skirt corresponds to the entire forge enveloped in white moonlight; her tin breasts to the anvil which, projected above the forge, reflects a greater intensity of light and has a breast-like shape. The movement of her arms in the agitated air may have been suggested by the heat waves which emanate from the forge and which are amplified by the action of the bellows. Thus there is a "natural" explanation for the child's fear that the moon's heart, i.e., the tin bathed in moonlight, will be made into jewelry (*GLR* 9, 1981, 116–17).

This is not my own response as I read the poem, even when prompted by the above suggestions. There is something un-Lorcan, I find, about such a reading. The magic is dispelled by fragmentation, logic and reality. Perhaps we are touching on an essential difference between Baroque poetry, where the fragmentation of an image in search of a logical explanation of each component part is justified, and twentieth-century imagery, where often it is not. The moon, I suggest, is a wholly visionary, magical figure — like the angels referred to earlier, like Walter de la Mare's moon ('Softly, silently now the moon / Walks the night in her silver shoon'), like the moon of traditional tales and nursery rhymes. The initial justification here lies in the popular superstition that the moon carries away children who look at it too much, and Lorca, appropriately adapting the superstition to an Andalusian context, presents the moon as a female dancer of death. The whiteness that is emphasised throughout the poem is thus a consequence of the basic image and requires no special, real-life explanation. Given the starting-point in local superstition, only two justifications are required: internal consistency (development in terms of a seductive female dancer) and emotive relevance (with emphasis on whiteness, coldness and hardness); in Lorca's own words, 'baile de amor y frío' (*A* I, 138). Both these requirements are fulfilled. Natural explanations are unnecessary and perhaps misplaced. I have yet to find an unlettered Andalusian who sees Lorca's angels as other than angels or his moon as other than a lunar dancer of death. In Lorca's neo-primitivism lies also a considerable part of his popular appeal.[19]

[19] With the above indicated emphasis on 'natural' explanations of Lorca's visionary figures one can compare similarly 'natural' responses to some of his other images and the associated neglect of less physical, but more important resonances (cf. above, pp. 39–40, examples from 'Thamar y Amnón').

'MARTIRIO DE SANTA OLALLA'

Poets synthesise; critics fragment. Aspects of Lorca's poetry that in the preceding pages have been isolated and studied out of context, in fact belong together, interacting with one another in a unique synthesis. Echoes of traditional ballads and Christian iconography, for example, join to enhance and to mythicise characters and actions. Nature, by its involvement, increases the effect. So do visionary figures. Despite the poet's emphasis on the here-and-now the overall effect is not realism but stylisation. In my companion volume I attempt to illustrate these things by the study of individual poems. Here I confine myself to a merely partial attempt by considering the opening lines of the 'Martirio de Santa Olalla' and indicating briefly the subsequent development of the poem in the light of my findings. Where I suggest the influence of Christian iconography I shall refer specifically to paintings in a collection that we know Lorca was familiar with: that bequeathed by Isabel the Catholic to the Cathedral of Granada.

The original title, 'Romance del martirio de la gitana Santa Olalla', suggests that Lorca, characteristically ahistoricist, saw the martyrdom as another means of elevating one of his gypsies, here by association with a popular saint. The poem opens with an evocation of Merida the night before the execution. A long-tailed horse runs through the street — possibly a river (Campbell) or a breeze (Loughran); more probably a horse that is also a visionary herald of the awaited killing (cf. 15: 29–30) — as soldiers dice or doze in careless insensitivity. In a pre-publication draft of line 3 Lorca wrote *juegan a los dados* but then changed it to *juegan o dormitan*. The earlier version makes clear a pointer to the Passion that we might otherwise overlook. In fifteenth-century Crucifixions the soldiers who cast lots for Christ's clothes (Matthew 27:35) are commonly depicted throwing dice and dice appear frequently in early Arma Christi along with three nails, a column and scourge, a lance, a sponge and other elements of the Crucifixion (cf. the *Mass of Saint Gregory* in Granada Cathedral; nine examples of dice also in Schiller, II, Figs. 658–774). Lorca presumably made the change in order to mute the parallel into mere suggestion, but also, more positively, in order to add *y dormitan* and thereby increase the effect of insensitivity. Besides, insensitive slumber at such a moment echoes a further biblical episode, also much represented in early painting: the sleep of the disciples during Christ's agony in the garden (Matthew 26:36–46; cf. Olalla's own agony, 15, and Botticelli's *Agony in the*

Garden, Granada). I drew attention in my preamble to Lorca's ahistoricism in fusing gypsy and early Christian martyr. If my present suggestion of biblical resonances is justified there is something similar in these lines, with the superposition of Christ's crucifixion on Olalla's martyrdom. The effect is to elevate and dignify her torment; also to detemporalise and universalise its significance.

Lorca turns now to the scene around (5–12). The *Minervas* are usually interpreted as olive trees (the tree of Minerva) or shrubs (regional usage). But as indicated earlier, Minerva was, among other things, a goddess of war and one of the great triad of Roman state divinities and I find in her leafless arms a reminder of the limbless statues of present-day Merida, a tacit contrast to Daphne's sprouting arms and, by the combination of the two, an image of the Roman empire's lost vitality. This impression of lost vitality is further reinforced by the suspended water, presumably frozen along the crests of the rocks (7–8), and the mutilation reappears in the night of recumbent torsos, suggesting both prostrate soldiers and limbless statues (a further indication of lost energies, especially in view of the funereal *yacentes*), and broken-nose stars (a cosmic echoing of the mutilated statues and, more widely, of Rome's own battered glory). Nature, then, both telluric and cosmic, participates in the scene. Merida's symbolic dark night of ruin awaits its final destruction with the coming of a new dawn: *aguarda grietas del alba / para derrumbarse toda.*

Amidst further echoes of the Passion — crowing cocks (13–14; cf. Memling's *Virgin and the Christ of Sorrows* in Granada), crown of thorns (20–2; cf. Van der Weyden's *Pietà* and Bouts's triptych of the Passion, both in Granada; here with juxtaposed suffering and the promise of new life), lance in the side (65–6; cf. the *Mass of St Gregory* and Memling's *Virgin and the Christ of Sorrows*, Granada) — it gradually becomes evident that it is Olalla's martyrdom that marks the coming of this new dawn. The change is heralded in the girl's wailing which shatters wineglasses (15–16). Thereafter, in Part II of the poem, it will become clearer. In contrast to the comatose and mutilated civilisation of Rome, with associated images of rigidity and lifelessness and freezing, Olalla's own mutilation is represented by gushing veins (26), streams of milk (38) and a thousand trickles of blood (39), all of which serve as it were to unfreeze the scene so far presented. Moreover, the *arroyos de leche* and *arbolillos de sangre* recall two of the most frequently represented Christian symbols of life: the Virgin's milk (cf. Memling's *The Virgin and Child of the Throne*, Granada) and Christ's

blood (cf. *The Mass of Saint Gregory*, Granada). Olalla's own milk and
blood, then, are not merely aspects of her martyrdom; they are also
pointers to the new life heralded by her martyrdom and they both flow
freely, appropriately accompanied by further pointers to new vitality:
sex likened to the trembling of an ensnared bird (29–30), leaping
manos cortadas (32) and defiant *arbolillos de sangre* (39–42). Olalla's
throat (*garganta*) which gushes blood seems clearly to prepare the way
for the later stream gorges (*gargantas de arroyo*) which, with the *agua
en vilo* unfrozen, presumably gush water (69), earlier images of leafless
arms and ensnared birds yield effectively to contrasting *ruiseñores en
ramos* (70), and the static and sterile whiteness of winter gives way to
leaping *vidrios de colores* (71) suggestive of both spring and apotheosis.
Whereas in his own poem on Eulalia's martyrdom Prudentius finally
distanced himself in time from the event to describe the saint's tomb
and its location, 'like a rose-covered meadow blushing with varied
blooms', the corresponding colours of Lorca's leaping *vidrios* appear as
a consequence of the martyrdom itself. Both martyrdom and poem
thus take on a wider significance than has hitherto been noted. The
'Martirio de Santa Olalla' is one of the most powerfully mythical
poems in *Romancero gitano*. Lorca's note on the manuscript of 'San
Gabriel' suggests that he at least would agree.

CONSTRUCTION AND PROGRESSION

The Poem

> El romance típico había sido siempre una narración y era lo na-
> rrativo lo que daba encanto a su fisonomía, porque, cuando se
> hacía lírico, sin eco de anécdota, se convertía en canción. Yo quise
> fundir el romance narrativo con el lírico sin que perdieran ninguna
> calidad (III, 341).

To illustrate the contrasting types of *romance* that Lorca here declares
as his starting-point, I quote the opening lines of representative poems:
one, an anonymous early narrative *romance*; the other, a twentieth-
century lyrical *romance* by Juan Ramón Jiménez:

En Ceuta está Julián,	moro viejo la escribía,
en Ceuta la bien nombrada:	y el conde se la notaba:
para las partes de aliende	después de haberla escrito,
quiere enviar su embajada;	al moro luego matara (*RVC* 4).

Yo no volveré. Y la noche
tibia, serena y callada,
dormirá el mundo, a los rayos
de su luna solitaria.

Mi cuerpo no estará allí,
y por la abierta ventana,
entrará una brisa fresca,
preguntando por mi alma.
(*Segunda antolojía poética*, 19)

On the one hand, a verb-guided linear succession of events narrated in
two-line periods; on the other, a more adjectival, lyrical description
and meditation evoked in four-line periods. And Lorca's aim was to
fuse the two. Among 'algunos poemas del *Romancero*' in which he felt
he had been successful he referred specifically to 'Romance sonámbulo'
and pointed to the main features of his fusion: the muting of narrative
into '*sensación* de anécdota', the incorporation of lyricism's resonances
and 'misterio poético', and the resulting 'agudo ambiente dramático'
(III, 341). It is these three aspects of his style with which we are here
principally concerned.

The first two can best be considered together, as Lorca himself
considered them in his lecture on Góngora. In the *Soledades*, he said,
Góngora's problem was to create a large-scale lyric poem. 'Pero ¿cómo
mantener una tensión lírica pura durante largos escuadrones de
versos? ¿Y cómo hacerlo sin narración? Si le daba a la narración, a la
anécdota, toda su importancia, se le convertía en épico al menor
descuido. Y si no narraba nada, el poema se rompía por mil partes sin
unidad ni sentido' (III, 243). Góngora, he continued, solved the pro-
blem by reducing narrative to a mere skeleton and enveloping it in 'la
carne magnífica de las imágenes' (III, 243). The anecdote thus loses its
importance, 'pero da con su hilo invisible *unidad* al poema', and
images take over, interacting with one another, 'ligadas a otras y a su
vez ligadas, y de ahí su aparente dificultad' (III, 243–4). Despite dif-
ferences of poem-length, line-length and imagery, Lorca, it seems, was
concerned with a similar problem and resolved it in a not wholly dis-
similar fashion.

I have considered the matter elsewhere and here confine myself to
brief observations on the poem adduced by Lorca himself, 'Romance
sonámbulo'. At her railing a girl awaits the return of her lover, ap-
parently away on a smuggling expedition. The lover arrives badly
wounded, goes up with the girl's father to where the girl was waiting
and finds her dead. Civil guards come to arrest him. This, it seems, is
the underlying anecdote and is generally accepted as such by critics.
But the evidence consists of mere suggestions: the boat, the horse,
the anxious waiting, the Andalusian and gypsy context, the wounded

lover, an apparent fight in the mountain passes, the father's distraught response, the arrival of civil guards and, from outside the poem, the Spanish system (until the 1950s) of both national and internal customs barriers, the smuggling tradition that was still very much alive in the first quarter of the twentieth century and Lorca's own indication of the presence somewhere in *Romancero gitano* (though he does not say where) of 'la nota vulgar del contrabandista' (III, 340). This has not convinced all critics and other interpretations have been proposed. Allen, for example, finds an underlying tale of marital infidelity involving the girl, her lover (wounded by the husband) and the husband himself (who has killed his wife, thrown her body into the storage tank and now, in insane revenge, shows her lover the corpse) and András proposes a story of civil guards who have forced their attentions on the girl during the lover's absence and now, in drunken revelry, come in search of further sexual favours.[1] Since there is only a '*sensación* de anécdota' we cannot be certain that they are wrong. What we can be certain about is that narrative itself is unimportant, that it serves at most merely as an 'hilo invisible' to solicit the reader's attention while the poem makes its impact and that, if there is an underlying 'nota vulgar del contrabandista', nothing *vulgar* remains. Pointers to a smuggling expedition are glimpsed only momentarily amidst a succession of dreamlike images. It is these, 'ligadas a otras y a su vez ligadas', that are important. As with Góngora, 'de ahí su aparente dificultad'.

At this point we return to another aspect of Lorca's lecture on Góngora and to the leitmotiv of my study: the interplay of 'núcleo central' and 'redondas perspectivas'. Amidst countless examples of such interplay one is central to 'Romance sonámbulo' and was considered in an earlier section: the colour green, its initial 'redonda perspectiva' of illusion, the threatening inroads of contradictory resonances of death, and thereafter a series of elements (the coming dawn, the wind, the fig-tree) where green is manifestly absent. Lorca produces the effect of a sleepwalking ballad by discarding mere anecdote and using his lyrical 'redondas perspectivas' as the main elements in the poem's progression. The result is not narrative but, as Lorca said of Góngora's poetry, 'tensión lírica'. The theme is yearning and lamenta-

---

[1] Rupert Allen, 'An analysis of narrative and symbol in Lorca's "Romance sonámbulo"', in *HR* 36 (1968), 338–52; Lásló András, 'El caso de la gitana sonámbula', in *Actas del Simposio Internacional de Estudios Hispánicos* [1976], Budapest 1978, 181–94.

tion, man's illusion and life's disillusion. Everything in the poem contributes to this; nothing is irrelevant. The final restatement of the opening lines echoes forlornly over a world of death and despair. By a sophisticated *rondeau* effect that emphasises the artistic completeness of the poem Lorca sets up the sort of resonances that modern writers are wont to find in the fragmentary incompleteness of some of the finest traditional *romances*.

I turn finally to the 'agudo ambiente dramático'. It is implicit in my previous paragraphs. The clear line of prosaic narrative is fragmented, but the essential dramatic elements remain: a girl's waiting, a young man's longing, an older man's distraught response, wounds and impending death, a procession of anguish, a fruitless quest, a flashback to earlier health and illusion, the girl's death, the irruptive civil guards. Like the 'pure poets' of his generation Lorca eliminates the prosaic and the anecdotic and concentrates attention on significant high points of experience. But whereas Guillén, for example, emphasised ecstatic peaks of personal delight in a world well made, Lorca emphasises high points of drama and tragedy in a world that is less well made and, being a dramatist, centres them not on himself but on others. The means by which he elevates these selected high points — stylisation, echoes of *cante*, incantatory repetition and variations on repetition, the involvement of nature, the interplay of images . . . — have been illustrated in previous pages and need not be repeated here. One new point, however, is relevant: like many other poems in the book 'Romance sonámbulo' is not only dramatic in tone; it is also comparable to drama in its progression, especially to Greek tragedy with the interplay of action and choric commentary. Thus: lines 1–12, choric prologue and first act; 13–24, commenting chorus with an incantatory pointer to wider resonances; 25–52, second act; 53–60, chorus with further commentary and broadening; 61–72, third act; 73–86, combined last act and choric epilogue. One finds something similar in almost all Lorca's *romances*, with associated dramatic techniques and corresponding dramatic detachment. In fusing the narrative *romance* with the lyrical *romance* Lorca created his own unique dramatic *romance*. It is an aspect of the work that merits further study.

The Book

The poems in *Romancero gitano* are not reproduced in the same order in which they were written.[2] In line with other poets of his generation, it seems, Lorca viewed his book not as a mere collection of poems but as a significantly structured, tonally unified and dynamically progressing artistic whole. There are suggestions of this in his lecture–recital: 'indudablemente la [obra] que hasta ahora tiene más unidad' (III, 339), 'la pureza de su construcción y el noble tono con que me esforcé al crearlo' (III, 340), 'El libro en conjunto [...] es el poema de Andalucía' (III, 340; with a revealing singular, as also in 'este poema' to refer to the whole book, III, 340). But the main evidence comes from the work itself. Except for a muted narrative link between the two Antoñito *romances* there is no anecdotic or chronological ordering of the type that one finds, for example, in the traditional *Romancero del Cid*. As in individual poems so also in the book as a whole, parallels, similarities and resonances seem to have guided the structure more than mere linear progression.

The work begins with two invented myths, said Lorca: the moon as a dancer of death and the wind as a satyr. These poems clearly belong together: by their common theme and similar treatment — a vulnerable human being beset by a personified force of nature —; also by the taking up at the beginning of Poem 2 (title and opening line) of both the *aire* and the *luna* with which Poem 1 concluded. Because of this juxtaposition and link, Preciosa's *luna de pergamino* immediately suggests that she too, like the moon (and like Cervantes's heroine), is both seductive and icily detached.

If one sees 'Reyerta' as mere anecdote it has little or no connection with Poems 1 and 2. But Lorca's comment points to something beyond mere anecdote: 'esa lucha sorda latente en Andalucía y en toda España de grupos que se atacan sin saber por qué, por causas misteriosas, por una mirada, por una rosa, porque un hombre de pronto siente un insecto sobre la mejilla, por un amor de hace dos siglos' (III, 343). Perhaps the black angels should be seen as angels of fate or evil, or

---

[2] The problem is complex and certain aspects are unclear. Basically, despite Lorca's own indication of 1924–27 as the period of composition, an early manuscript of *RG* 17 is dated 28 December 1921 and there is evidence that other poems too — probably *RG* 1, 4 and 7 (written up in manuscripts dated 29 July, 2 August and 30 July 1924 respectively) — existed in early versions by the autumn of 1923 (José Mora Guarnido, *FGL y su mundo*, Buenos Aires 1958, pp. 209–10, and, on the echoing of a discarded 1921 poem in *RG* 4 and 7, Christian de Paepe, ed., FGL, *Poema del cante jondo*, Madrid 1986, pp. 7–8, 314). For the fullest survey of relevant chronology, see *4*, 161–94.

spirits of discord like Alberti's 'ángeles bélicos', or possibly, like classical harpies, souls of the dead that snatch away those of the living. The poem would then be thematically akin to the previous two, with another indication of man's suffering at the hands of dark forces beyond his control, and 'Romance sonámbulo' would follow on naturally, with emphasis — if my interpretation is correct — on the all-pervading panorama of man's illusion and life's disillusion.

Illusion and disillusion continue, with specific examples in the following three poems: first 'La monja gitana', with vitality and repression already implicit in the title and a protagonist who embroiders simple flowers, dreams of the more colourful flowers that she would like to embroider but finally returns to her modest task; then, on a more humorous plane that relaxes tension while making the same point, 'La casada infiel' in which a gypsy Don Juan tells of an amatory escapade and let-down; finally, with a 'sensación de anécdota' akin to 'Romance sonámbulo' and a similar sense of mystery and despair, the 'Romance de la pena negra', on Soledad Montoya's fruitless quest for escape from darkness. If it is true, as is commonly stated, that the underlying anecdote here is of love and abandonment, this might further explain the poem's juxtaposition to 'La casada infiel' — not of course to suggest that Soledad is the 'casada infiel', but as an echo of abandonment seen from another viewpoint.

The next three poems, the archangel poems, are at the centre of the book and, like panels in an altar triptych, they clearly belong together. 'San Miguel', with its emphasis on lost vitality, serves nicely — as 'San Gabriel', for example, would not — as a transition from the preceding poems; 'San Rafael', at the centre, is significantly a tribute to Góngora, and 'San Gabriel' completes the triptych with an Annunciation scene that introduces elements to be echoed in the following poems.

At first sight the Antoñito poems (11 and 12) have no connection with 'San Gabriel'. But no two gypsies in the book are more alike than Saint Gabriel and Antoñito, and Lorca's neo-primitive evocation of the Annunciation in Poem 10 is balanced by corresponding pointers to the Passion in 11 and 12. Moreover, the *tres golpes de sangre* of which Antoñito dies (12:41) are surely an echo of the *tres balas de almendra verde* that trembled in the voice of the unborn gypsy Christ child (10:65) — and, of course, of the symbolic three nails of the Crucifixion. Biblical and iconographic resonances continue in the next poem, significantly entitled 'Muerto de amor', and the 'Romance del emplazado' appears, in context, almost as a reminder of judgment day. But, except between Poems 11 and 12, there is no question of any linear, narrative link. Lorca offers, at most, mere suggestions and resonances. And the overall effect, once more, is of illusion yielding to disillusion: from the promise of the Annunciation, the high point — and almost only point — of optimism in the book, to death in innocence (12) and in love (13) and the tormenting solitude of the awaited judgment day whose only consolations are dignity and *descanso* (14). In the epic 'Romance de la Guardia Civil española' biblical and iconographic resonances continue, but there is greater emphasis now on the real-life world of the gypsy. Appropriately, after the judgment of Poem 14, civil guards execute their own last judgment and destroy the gypsy world of illusion that has been seeking expression throughout the book. Amidst devastation and slaughter the *ciudad de los gitanos* is finally left only as an image within the poet himself.

The 'tres romances históricos' form a concluding triptych to balance the earlier triptych of archangels. They have nothing to do with gypsies, but Lorca's references to 'la gitana Santa Olalla' (III, 901) and to *vírgenes gitanas* (18:86) suggest why they appear: as a broadening of the gypsy experience in time and space and significance: persecution (16), futile quest for illusion (17), fate and violence (18). Along with Poems 1 and 2 these are the most mythical in the book. But whereas in the opening poems mythical figures (moon, wind) and humans (child, Preciosa) merely coexist, in the last three poems it is as though humans themselves attain mythical stature: Olalla as the bringer of new life, Don Pedro as the quester after illusion, Thamar and Amnón as participants in a cosmic conflict that results in the final violation not only of the seductive but frigid, moon-bathed Thamar but also of the seductive and frigid moon itself with which the book opened.

THE PRESENT TEXT

In preparing the text of *Romancero gitano* I have paid special attention to the first edition (Revista de Occidente, 1928), the typographically reset but otherwise virtually identical second edition (Revista de Occidente, 1929), the fifth edition (Espasa-Calpe, 1935), the eighth edition (Espasa-Calpe, 1937), Guillermo de Torre's *Obras completas* edition (Losada, 1938), Arturo del Hoyo's *Obras completas* edition (Aguilar, 22nd ed., 1986) and the recent editions by Mario Hernández (Alianza, 2nd ed., 1983) and Miguel García Posada (Akal, 1982). I have also consulted Mario Hernández's notes on the fourth edition, which he believes to be identical to the third. Finally, I have consulted manuscript versions of individual poems, most notably the facsimiles published by Rafael Martínez Nadal, and all known pre-*RG* published versions.

Except for six points on which I append endnotes the only differences between the eight editions that I have examined personally are of punctuation, typography and printing error. The 1928 and 1929 Aguilar and García Posada editions, for example, do not insert dashes to indicate speech; the 1935, 1937, 1938 and Hernández editions do, though with occasional omissions. Lorca's extant manuscripts offer no clear guidance, being generally early, scantily punctuated and inconsistent: at times speech is indicated by means of inverted commas, at times not at all, at yet others with both inverted commas and non-indication within the same poem (*A* I, 138). Pre-1928 published versions are better punctuated but not clearer in their guidance: 'Romance de la luna, luna', for example, appeared in *El Norte de Castilla* (1926) and *Verso y Prosa* (1927) with inverted commas; 'Reyerta', in *La Verdad* (1926) and *L'Amic de les Arts* (1927) with no speech indications; 'Muerto de amor', in *Litoral* (1927) with no speech indications in the first half of the poem and inverted commas in the second half. In support of the non-indication of speech it has been argued that this was usual in traditional *romance* collections and that Lorca probably wished to emphasise the traditional character of his poems by doing likewise. But speech dashes were included both in the best known *romance* collection of Lorca's day, *Romances viejos castellanos (Primavera y flor de romances)* edited by Wolf, Hofmann and Menéndez y Pelayo, and in the collection that was shortly to surpass *Romances viejos castellanos* in popularity, Menéndez Pidal's *Flor nueva de romances viejos*, first published — like *Romancero gitano* — in 1928. Moreover, whatever the explanation of the absence of speech indications in the 1928 and 1929 editions, *guiones* were used in the 1935 edition (and in the 1933 and 1934 editions, *4*, 14–15) and it seems reasonable to assume that this was at Lorca's instigation or at least not contrary to his wishes. Finally, speech dashes aid understanding. I therefore use them in the present text.

The eccentric use of commas in the 1928 and 1929 editions poses a more difficult problem. In 'Romance de la Guardia Civil española', for example, one finds: *Un caballo malherido, / llamaba a todas las puertas* (29–30), *El viento, vuelve desnudo / la esquina de la sorpresa* (33–4), *La media luna, soñaba / un éxtasis de cigüeña* (49–50), *Un rumor de siemprevivas, / invade las cartucheras* (67–8), *La ciudad libre de miedo, / multiplicaba sus puertas* (73–4), *Por las calles de penumbra, / huyen las gitanas viejas* (85–6), *En el Portal de Belén, / los gitanos se congregan* (93–4), *Rosa la de los Camborios, / gime sentada en su puerta* (105–6). These commas, one feels, can hardly have been added by the publisher. Given Lorca's scant use of commas in most of his early manuscripts, including a manuscript that contains the last four examples (all without a comma, *A* I, 196–203), it is tempting to imagine him reading through his final version before submission, savouring each word and group of words, responding to the resonances, and introducing commas not as a grammarian but as a poet, in order to indicate pauses and thereby encourage his reader also to savour words and respond to resonances. The commas would thus be poetically relevant. But Lorca's judgment of poetic relevance seems to have changed from one version of the poem to another. In November 1926, for example, in a letter to Guillén, he quoted a fairly definitive version of lines 9–62 that included the first three examples listed above, all without a comma, but offered two anomalous commas that did not appear in 1928: *por donde pasan ordenan, / silencios de goma oscura* and *los gitanos en sus fraguas, / forjaban soles y flechas* (III, 899–900). One finds similar inconsistencies elsewhere: between manuscript and 1928 edition:

En la ribera del mar,	En la ribera del mar
no hay palma que se le iguale	no hay palma que se le iguale,
ni Emperador coronado (*A* I,	ni Emperador coronado
160)	(1928)

between manuscript and pre-1928 publication:

Los ojos en las umbrías,	Los ojos en las umbrías
se empañan de inmensa noche	se empañan de inmensa noche
(III, 894)[3]	(*Litoral*, 1)

between different pre-1928 published versions:

las navajas de Albacete	las navajas de Albacete
bellas de sangre contraria,	bellas, de sangre contraria,
(*La Verdad*, 59; 1926)	(*L'Amic de les Arts*,
	15; 1927)

---

[3] The *OC* edition, here as elsewhere, has changed the punctuation. I therefore give page references to *OC* but quote from Jorge Guillén, *Federico en persona*, Buenos Aires 1959, p. 100.

and between pre-1928 published version and 1928 edition:

Angeles negros traían,   Angeles negros traían
pañuelos y agua de nieve   pañuelos y agua de nieve
(*L'Amic de les Arts*, 15;   (1928)
1927)

One finds also, in 1928, unusual comma usage balanced by unusual comma omission: *ella sueña en su baranda / verde carne, pelo verde* (4:6–7), *cierra sus ojos de azogue / dando a la quieta penumbra* (8:10– 11), *Anunciación de los Reyes / bien lunada y mal vestida* (10:27–8) . . ., as well as inconsistency within the same poem, even where lines are repeated: *Antonio Torres Heredia, / hijo y nieto de Camborios* (11:1–2), *Antonio Torres Heredia / hijo y nieto de Camborios* (11: 25–6). The necessary inference from all this — and from a host of similar evidence — is that, if Lorca did use commas for their poetic relevance, he was singularly flexible. One therefore looks with special attention to the reset and revised edition of 1935. Here the punctuation of 1928 and 1929 was almost totally regularised, most notably with the elimination of anomalous commas at the end of a line (as in *Dentro de la fragua el niño, / tiene los ojos cerrados*, where there was in any case no comma in the extant manuscript, *A* I, 140, or in either pre-1928 published version). This elimination does not destroy the effect of the 1928 commas, for the line-ending creates its own pause and stress. In any case, Lorca was presumably involved in the revision. I have therefore eliminated such commas where this is justified by the 1935 edition. But the 1928 edition had also seven cases of anomalous comma within the line (of the type *El viento, vuelve desnudo*). Four were deleted in 1935 (13:35, 15:33, 15:49, 18:89); two were retained in 1935 but deleted in 1937 (4:64, 7:20); one was retained in both 1935 and 1937, with the addition of an earlier comma to create a parenthesis and thus normalise usage (18:41). Pre-*RG* versions (manuscript and published), in so far as they exist, offer conflicting guidance: with no comma in manuscripts and a comma in the only pre-*RG* published version (13:35; *Litoral*). In the belief that Lorca, despite inconsistencies, did find the 1928 punctuation poetically significant — and since there is no line-ending in these seven cases to bring out the pause — I accept the 1928 reading but list the examples so that the reader can delete them if he wishes.[4]

---

[4] With the above seven cases I have not listed 13:10 (identically punctu-ated in *Litoral*), for I see the construction as different, more akin to 7:5 and

The above two problems account for most of the textual variants in the eight editions indicated. The majority of others are easily resolved: various aspects of typographical practice (accents on such words as *fué* and *vió*, the indenting of the first line of a verse or section, the printing of the first word of a poem in capitals, etc.); occasional printing and editorial errors (for example, *horzas* for *orzas* and *maniquíes* for *maniquís* in 1928 and 1929, and the loss of an asterisk and space at the bottom of a page in 1929 and the failure of subsequent editors to realise that there should be both asterisk and space); Guillermo de Torre's now outdated omission of all dedications because some of those named were right-wing .... Here as with the other points mentioned above — and as with a number of other generally minor punctuation problems — I have usually made my choice without comment, guided by modern typographical practice, a desire for clarity and, very especially, respect for Lorca's texts as they appeared in the poet's lifetime. The line numbering of course is my own — to aid reference.

7:7 and with a similar fusing of real plane and evoked plane. The use of the comma is thus not anomalous.

As further evidence of Lorca's use of punctuation to encourage resonances one can compare 4:3–4 with 4:85–6 where the resonances have become more important. I find 1:29–30 significant too. One of the two extant manuscripts and both pre-*RG* printed versions have exclamation marks in both lines: ¡*Cómo canta la zumaya!* / ¡*Ay, cómo canta en el árbol!* (*El Norte de Castilla*, 9 April 1926; *Verso y Prosa* 7, July 1927). This is in accordance with typographical practice and it is tempting to accept the reading. But there are no first-line exclamation marks in the other manuscript or in any edition published in Lorca's lifetime. I therefore omit them. It seems at least probable that Lorca wanted to emphasise the crescendo effect, with moderately exclamatory *Cómo* ... (29) succeeded by dramatically exclamatory ¡*Ay, cómo* ...! (30).

SELECT BIBLIOGRAPHY

Emphasis is on works of synthesis, either on a given aspect of *Romancero gitano* or on the book as a whole. Commentary-based studies are in general reserved for the bibliography in my companion volume, *Federico García Lorca's 'Romancero gitano'. Eighteen Commentaries* (Manchester University Press, 1988), but may be included here if they seem especially significant in range or findings. Abbreviations: (F)GL, (Federico) García Lorca; *RG*; *Romancero gitano*; *A* I, *Autógrafos*, I (the third item below); *RVC*, *Romances viejos castellanos*; *RC*, *Romancero del Cid*; *RGen*, *Romancero general* (details of all three on p. 19); UP, University Press; those referring to periodicals are in accordance with *The Year's Work in Modern Language Studies*.

BASIC TEXTS

Federico García Lorca, *Obras completas*, Madrid: Aguilar, 22nd ed., 3 vols., 1986 [Unless otherwise stated, Lorca page references are to this edition].

——, '*Romancero gitano*' (1935–36], in *OC* III, 339–46 [Lorca's own invaluable commented reading].

——, *Autógrafos*, I (*Facsímiles de ochenta y siete poemas y tres prosas*), ed. Rafael Martínez Nadal, Oxford: Dolphin, 1975 [Facsimiles and transcription of pre-publication manuscripts, at times only fragmentary; includes, in part at least, *RG* poems 1, 5, 6, 7, 9, 10, 13, 14, 15, 16, 18; hereafter abbreviated *A* I].

ANNOTATED EDITIONS OF *RG*

1. FGL, *Poema del cante jondo, RG*, ed. Allen Josephs and Juan Caballero, Madrid: Cátedra, 1977 [*RG* study, 77–121; *RG* text (mingling of 1928 and Aguilar) with copious footnotes, 225–302].

2. FGL, *Œuvres complètes*, ed. André Belamich, Gallimard, La Pléiade, 1981 [*RG* text in French, 417–52; *RG* study and notes (textual and explanatory), 1393–1431].

3. FGL, *Poesía*, 2, ed. Miguel García-Posada, Madrid: Akal, 1982 [*RG* study, 11–41; *RG* text (basically 1928), 141–85; *RG* notes (textual), 693–701].

4. FGL, *RG*, ed. Mario Hernández [1981], Madrid: Alianza, 2nd ed., 1983 [Study, 9–46; text (basically but critically 1934), 49–103; chronology, 161–94; notes (textual), 197–210].

CRITICAL STUDIES (in chronological order of first publication)

5. Melchor Fernández Almagro, 'FGL: *RG*', in *RO* 21 (July–September 1928), 373–8 [The best contemporary review: elevation of gypsy world to level of epic and myth].

6. Angel del Río, *Vida y obras de FGL* [1941], Zaragoza: Estudios Literarios, 1952, pp. 78–87 [Interplay of 'lo popular' and 'lo culto'].

7. Arturo Barea, *Lorca, el poeta y su pueblo* [1944], Buenos Aires: Losada, 1956 [Lorca expresses the ordinary Spaniard's feelings about oppression, sex and death. The final chapter, 'El poeta y su arte', is absent from the 1944 English edition].

8. Arturo Barea, 'Las raíces del lenguaje poético de Lorca', in *BSS* 22 (1945), 3–15 (4–8 on *RG*) [Popular sources of Lorca's imagery].

9. Guillermo Díaz-Plaja, *FGL* [1948], Buenos Aires: Austral, 1954, pp. 37–56, 106–40 [A valuable pioneering work, especially on sources; not wholly outdated. Brief comments on all *RG* poems].

10. C. M. Bowra, *The Creative Experiment*, London: Macmillan, 1949, pp. 1–28 [Good on the modern movement in general], 189–219 [Brief comments on most *RG* poems].

11. Daniel Devoto, 'Notas sobre el elemento tradicional en la obra de GL' [1950], in *39*, 115–64 [A pioneer work on the presence of popular lines, images, expressions, etc.; relatively little on *RG* (part of 139–46)].

12. Juan López-Morillas, 'GL y el primitivismo lírico: reflexiones sobre el *RG*' [1950], in *39*, 287–99 [Lorca's gypsy symbolises primitive man; his violence is a reaction to his sense of lost liberty].

13. Roy Campbell, *Lorca. An Appreciation of his Poetry*, Cambridge: Bowes & Bowes, 1952, pp. 7–24 ('The Regional Poet'), 40–61 ('The *RG*') [Emphasises local roots and Baroque influence; good renderings into ballad metre, though often only extracts; brief comments on most *RG* poems].

14. J. L. Flecniakoska, *L'univers poétique de FGL*, Bordeaux: Bière, 1952 [A general survey, with emphasis on *RG*: senses, imagery, themes, rhythms].

15. Angel Alvarez de Miranda, *La metáfora y el mito* [1953], Madrid: Taurus, 1963 [Myth in Lorca's poetry. A basic study].

16. Concha Zardoya, *Poesía española contemporánea*, Madrid: Guadarrama, 1961, pp. 335–96 ('La técnica metafórica de FGL' [1954]) [Classification of Lorca's metaphors, with pointers to the categories most relevant to *RG*].

17. Jaroslaw M. Flys, *El lenguaje poético de FGL*, Madrid: Gredos, 1955 [Stylistic study, with emphasis on Lorca's use of metaphor and symbol].

18. Gino L. Rizzo, 'Poesía de FGL y poesía popular', in *Clavileño* 36 (November–December 1955), 44–51 [Lorca's use of popular sources].

19. Pedro Salinas, *Ensayos de literatura hispánica*, Madrid: Aguilar, 3rd ed., 1967, pp. 349–53 ('El romancismo y el siglo xx: FGL' [1955]) [The importance of metaphor in the transition from the here-and-now to enigma, myth and the supernatural].

20. Jean-Louis Schonberg, *FGL. L'homme. L'œuvre*, Paris: Plon, 1956, pp. 186–211 [Brief comments on all *RG* poems].

21. Gustavo Correa, *La poesía mítica de FGL*, Eugene: Oregon UP, 1957, pp. 22–53 [A landmark in Lorca studies, with myth-emphasising commentaries on all *RG* poems].

22. Christoph Eich, *FGL, poeta de la intensidad*, Madrid: Gredos, 1958 [Temporal structure in FGL, with emphasis on the Spanish intensity and *garbo* of the present moment].

23. Albert Henry, *Les grands poèmes andalous de FGL*, Ghent: Romanica Gandensia 6, 1958, 217–46 ('Récit et poésie dans le *RG*') [Comments on most *RG* poems].

24. Allen W. Phillips, 'Sobre la poética de GL', in *RHM* 24 (1958), 36–48 [A survey of Lorca's pronouncements on poetics, with emphasis on the interplay of inspiration/spontaneity/*duende* and conscious artistry/effort/control].

25. Reyes Carbonell, *Espíritu de llama*, Pittsburgh: Duquesne UP, 1962, pp. 101–20 ('Musicalidad plástica en la poesía de FGL') [Sound imagery in *RG*].

26. Juan Cano Ballesta, 'Una veta reveladora en la poesía de GL: los tiempos del verbo y sus matices expresivos' [1965], in *39*, 45–75 [A perceptive *RG*-based study; nicely supplemented by *34*].

27. Carl W. Cobb, *FGL*, New York: Twayne, 1967, pp. 58–78 [Comments on all *RG* poems].

28. Marie Laffranque, *Les idées esthétiques de FGL*, Paris: Centre de recherches hispaniques, 1967 [Surveys Lorca's development as a conscious theorist of his art, with emphasis on lectures and letters; for *RG* see especially Chapter 4].

29. Carlos Ramos-Gil, *Claves líricas de GL. Ensayos sobre la expresión y los climas poéticas lorquianos*, Madrid: Aguilar, 1967 [Lorca's poetry in general, with special emphasis on the presence of death and dark forces].

30. Tomás Navarro Tomás, *Los poetas en sus versos: desde Jorge Manrique a GL*, Barcelona: Ariel, 1973, pp. 355–78 ('La intuición rítmica en FGL' [1968]) [Lorca's subtle exploitation of *romance* rhythms].

31. Francisco Umbral, *Lorca, poeta maldito*, Madrid: Biblioteca Nueva, 1968, pp. 95–125 ('Los gitanos'), 127–31 ('Andalucía y surrealismo') [Reflexions — usually psychological or sociological — on most *RG* poems].

32. Beverly J. DeLong, 'Sobre el desarrollo lorquiano del romance tradicional', in *Hispanófila* 35 (January 1969), 51–62 [*RG* and the traditional *romance*: similarities and differences].

33. Juan Antonio Rivas López, 'GL, ¿un poeta popular?', in *Los estudiantes de ciencias a FGL*, Universidad de Granada, 1969, pp. 123–40 [Popular sources, but with elevation to universal significance].

34. Joseph Szertics, 'FGL y el romancero viejo: los tiempos verbales y su alternancia', in *MLN* 84 (1969), 269–85 [The expressivity of verb-tense interplay in *RG*].

35. C. B. Morris, *A Generation of Spanish Poets 1920–1936*, Cambridge UP, 1971 [Includes pages on *RG*, with emphasis on Lorca's indebtedness to popular poetry].

36. Carlos Edmundo de Ory, 'Salvador Rueda y GL', in *CHA* 255 (March 1971), 417–44 (esp. 438–43) [Finds many echoes of Rueda in *RG*; convincing].

37. Richard L. Predmore, 'Simbolismo ambiguo en la poesía de GL', in *PSA* 63 (October-December 1971), 229–40 [Ambiguity as an expressive device, with special reference to the duality of love and death in five symbols: *caballo, luna, viento, manzana, sombra*].

38. Carlos Feal Deibe, *Eros y Lorca*, Barcelona: EDHASA, 1973,

pp. 63–71, 129–228 [*RG* 1, 2, 3, 6, 8, 11 and 12 on the Freudian couch].

39. Ildefonso-Manuel Gil (ed.), *FGL*, Madrid: Taurus, 1973 [A valuable collection of previously published studies, including several relevant to *RG*: *11*, *12*, *26* (above) and others].

40. Antonio Lara Pozuelo, *El adjetivo en la lírica de FGL*, Barcelona: Ariel, 1973 [Includes a poem-by-poem survey of adjective use in *RG*].

41. Alfred Rodríguez and Jack E. Tomlins, 'Notas para una relección del *RG*', in *RoN* 15 (1973–74), 541–5 [Critics' over-exclusive emphasis on myth should be moderated by greater attention to popular influences].

42. Francisco Mena Benito, *El tradicionalismo de FGL*, Barcelona: Rondas, 1974 [Lorca as a continuer and renovator of the *romance* tradition; comprehensive stylistic comparison of *RG* and the traditional *romance*; underplays the differences].

43. K. M. Sibbald, 'FGL's original contributions to the literary magazines in the years 1917–1937', in *GLR* 2, no. 1 (Spring 1974), n.p. [Includes the fullest available survey of differences between pre-*RG* published versions of *RG* poems and the 1969 Aguilar text (slightly changed in 1986)].

44. Alice M. Pollin, *A Concordance to the Plays and Poems of FGL*, Ithaca: Cornell UP, 1975 [An invaluable reference work for Lorca studies].

45. C. B. Morris, '*Bronce y sueño*: Lorca's gypsies', in *Neophilologus* 61 (1977), 227–44 [Emphasises Lorca's idealising vision].

46. Juan Cano Ballesta, 'Utopía y rebelión contra un mundo alienante: el *RG* de Lorca', in *GLR* 6 (1978), 71–85 [Finds a Marx-like gypsy Utopia in conflict with the 'organismo estatal' represented by the Civil Guard].

47. David K. Loughran, *FGL. The Poetry of Limits*, London: Tamesis, 1978, pp. 135–63 [Commentaries on *RG* 2, 5, 7, 11, 12, 14, 15, 16, 17].

48. Felipe Pedraza Jiménez, 'Símbolo e imagen en el *RG*', in *Insula* 380–1 (July–August 1978), 21 [The importance of the evoked plane in its own right, with its multiple resonances].

49. Alfredo Rodríguez, 'GL, los gitanos y la Guardia Civil', in *Hispanófila* 64 (September 1978), 61–9 [Gypsies and Civil Guard as polarised symbols of anarchy and rigid order].

50. J. M. Aguirre, 'Zorrilla y GL: leyendas y romances gitanos', in *BH* 81 (1979), 75–92 [Lorca's admiration; Z's possible influence, especially the idealised gypsy and the nun in *RG* 5].

51. Andrew P. Debicki, 'Códigos expresivos en el *RG*', in *Texto Crítico* 14 (1979), 143–54 [Literal and metaphorical levels of meaning interact and give force to *RG*].

52. Juan Manuel Rozas and Gregorio Torres Nebrera, *El grupo poético del 27*, Madrid: Cincel, 1980, pp. 12–22 [A good brief study of *RG*].

53. Derek Harris, 'The theme of the Crucifixion in Lorca's *RG*', in *BHS* 58 (1981), 329–38 [With special reference to *RG* 10, 11, 12, 17].

54. James E. Larkins, 'Myth upon myth: five animals of the *RG*', in *Hispania* 64 (1981), 14–22 [Mythological significance of the dove, bear, unicorn, satyr and dog].

55. John Crosbie, 'Structure and counter-structure in Lorca's *RG*', in *MLR* 77 (1982), 74–88 [Sophisticated imagery, with multiple but related meanings; centred on the gypsy/civil guard antithesis].

56. Carl W. Cobb, *Lorca's 'RG'. A Ballad Translation and Critical Study*, Jackson: Mississippi UP, 1983 [All *RG* poems: translation, commentary and general study].

57. José Carlos Lisboa, *Verde que te quero verde (Ensaio de interpretação do 'RG')*, Rio de Janeiro: Zahar, 1983 [Extensive commentaries on all *RG* poems].

58. Enrique López Castellón, Introduction to his edition of *RG*, Madrid: Busma, 1983, pp. 9–23 [Comments briefly on all *RG* poems].

59. Derek Harris, 'El *RG* o el baile de burlas y veras', in *Las Nuevas Letras* (Almeria) 2 (Spring 1985), 42–51 [*Cultismo*; includes commentary on *RG* 2].

60. Luis Beltrán Fernández de los Ríos, *La arquitectura del humo: una reconstrucción del 'RG' de FGL*, London: Tamesis, 1986 [Expansive commentary on all *RG* poems].

61. Andrew P. Debicki, 'Metonimia, metáfora y mito en el *RG*', in *CHA* 435–6 (September–October 1986), 609–18 [Metonymy commonly underlies metaphor in *RG* and explains its poetic impact].

ROMANCERO GITANO

1
ROMANCE DE LA LUNA, LUNA

A Conchita García Lorca

La luna vino a la fragua
con su polisón de nardos.
El niño la mira, mira.
El niño la está mirando.
5   En el aire conmovido
mueve la luna sus brazos
y enseña, lúbrica y pura,
sus senos de duro estaño.
—Huye luna, luna, luna.
10   Si vinieran los gitanos,
harían con tu corazón
collares y anillos blancos.
—Niño, déjame que baile.
Cuando vengan los gitanos,
15   te encontrarán sobre el yunque
con los ojillos cerrados.
—Huye luna, luna, luna,
que ya siento sus caballos.
—Niño, déjame, no pises
20   mi blancor almidonado.

El jinete se acercaba
tocando el tambor del llano.
Dentro de la fragua el niño
tiene los ojos cerrados.

25   Por el olivar venían,
bronce y sueño, los gitanos.

Las cabezas levantadas
y los ojos entornados.

Cómo canta la zumaya,
30 ¡ay, cómo canta en el árbol!
Por el cielo va la luna
con un niño de la mano.

Dentro de la fragua lloran,
dando gritos, los gitanos.
35 El aire la vela, vela.
El aire la está velando.

2
PRECIOSA Y EL AIRE

A Dámaso Alonso

Su luna de pergamino
Preciosa tocando viene,
por un anfibio sendero
de cristales y laureles.
5 El silencio sin estrellas,
huyendo del sonsonete,
cae donde el mar bate y canta
su noche llena de peces.
En los picos de la sierra
10 los carabineros duermen
guardando las blancas torres
donde viven los ingleses.
Y los gitanos del agua
levantan, por distraerse,
15 glorietas de caracolas
y ramas de pino verde.

*

Su luna de pergamino
Preciosa tocando viene.
Al verla se ha levantado
20 el viento, que nunca duerme.
San Cristobalón desnudo,
lleno de lenguas celestes,
mira a la niña tocando
una dulce gaita ausente.

25   —Niña, deja que levante
      tu vestido para verte.
      Abre en mis dedos antiguos
      la rosa azul de tu vientre.

      Preciosa tira el pandero
30   y corre sin detenerse.
      El viento-hombrón la persigue
      con una espada caliente.

      Frunce su rumor el mar.
      Los olivos palidecen.
35   Cantan las flautas de umbría
      y el liso gong de la nieve.

      ¡Preciosa, corre, Preciosa,
      que te coge el viento verde!
      ¡Preciosa, corre, Preciosa!
40   ¡Míralo por dónde viene!
      Sátiro de estrellas bajas
      con sus lenguas relucientes.

                    *

    . Preciosa, llena de miedo,
      entra en la casa que tiene,
45   más arriba de los pinos,
      el cónsul de los ingleses.

      Asustados por los gritos
      tres carabineros vienen,
      sus negras capas ceñidas
50   y los gorros en las sienes.

      El inglés da a la gitana
      un vaso de tibia leche,

y una copa de ginebra
que Preciosa no se bebe.

55   Y mientras cuenta, llorando,
su aventura a aquella gente,
en las tejas de pizarra
el viento, furioso, muerde.

3
REYERTA

A Rafael Méndez

En la mitad del barranco
las navajas de Albacete,
bellas de sangre contraria,
relucen como los peces.
5 Una dura luz de naipe
recorta en el agrio verde
caballos enfurecidos
y perfiles de jinetes.
En la copa de un olivo
10 lloran dos viejas mujeres.
El toro de la reyerta
se sube por las paredes.
Angeles negros traían
pañuelos y agua de nieve.
15 Angeles con grandes alas
de navajas de Albacete.
Juan Antonio el de Montilla
rueda muerto la pendiente,
su cuerpo lleno de lirios
20 y una granada en las sienes.
Ahora monta cruz de fuego
carretera de la muerte.

*

El juez, con guardia civil,
por los olivares viene.
25 Sangre resbalada gime

muda canción de serpiente.
—Señores guardias civiles:
aquí pasó lo de siempre.
Han muerto cuatro romanos
30 y cinco cartagineses.

*

La tarde loca de higueras
y de rumores calientes
cae desmayada en los muslos
heridos de los jinetes.
35 Y ángeles negros volaban
por el aire de poniente.
Angeles de largas trenzas
y corazones de aceite.

4

ROMANCE SONAMBULO

A Gloria Giner
y
A Fernando de los Ríos

Verde que te quiero verde.
Verde viento. Verdes ramas.
El barco sobre la mar
y el caballo en la montaña.
5 Con la sombra en la cintura,
ella sueña en su baranda,
verde carne, pelo verde,
con ojos de fría plata.
Verde que te quiero verde.
10 Bajo la luna gitana,
las cosas la están mirando
y ella no puede mirarlas.

*

Verde que te quiero verde.
Grandes estrellas de escarcha
15 vienen con el pez de sombra
que abre el camino del alba.
La higuera frota su viento
con la lija de sus ramas,
y el monte, gato garduño,
20 eriza sus pitas agrias.
Pero ¿quién vendrá? ¿Y por dónde? ...
Ella sigue en su baranda,

verde carne, pelo verde,
soñando en la mar amarga.

                    *

25   —Compadre, quiero cambiar
mi caballo por su casa,
mi montura por su espejo,
mi cuchillo por su manta.
Compadre, vengo sangrando,
30   desde los puertos de Cabra.
—Si yo pudiera, mocito,
este trato se cerraba.
Pero yo ya no soy yo,
ni mi casa es ya mi casa.
35   —Compadre, quiero morir
decentemente en mi cama.
De acero, si puede ser,
con las sábanas de holanda.
¿No ves la herida que tengo
40   desde el pecho a la garganta?
—Trescientas rosas morenas
lleva tu pechera blanca.
Tu sangre rezuma y huele
alrededor de tu faja.
45   Pero yo ya no soy yo,
ni mi casa es ya mi casa.
—Dejadme subir al menos
hasta las altas barandas,
¡dejadme subir!, dejadme
50   hasta las verdes barandas.
Barandales de la luna
por donde retumba el agua.

                    *

Ya suben los dos compadres
hacia las altas barandas.
55 Dejando un rastro de sangre.
Dejando un rastro de lágrimas.
Temblaban en los tejados
farolillos de hojalata.
Mil panderos de cristal
60 herían la madrugada.

*

Verde que te quiero verde,
verde viento, verdes ramas.
Los dos compadres subieron.
El largo viento, dejaba
65 en la boca un raro gusto
de hiel, de menta y de albahaca.
—¡Compadre! ¿Dónde está, dime,
dónde está tu niña amarga?
—¡Cuántas veces te esperó!
70 ¡Cuántas veces te esperara,
cara fresca, negro pelo,
en esta verde baranda!

*

Sobre el rostro del aljibe
se mecía la gitana.
75 Verde carne, pelo verde,
con ojos de fría plata.
Un carámbano de luna
la sostiene sobre el agua.
La noche se puso íntima
80 como una pequeña plaza.
Guardias civiles borrachos
en la puerta golpeaban.

Verde que te quiero verde.
Verde viento. Verdes ramas.
85 El barco sobre la mar.
Y el caballo en la montaña.

5
LA MONJA GITANA

A José Moreno Villa

Silencio de cal y mirto.
Malvas en las hierbas finas.
La monja borda alhelíes
sobre una tela pajiza.
5   Vuelan en la araña gris
siete pájaros del prisma.
La iglesia gruñe a lo lejos
como un oso panza arriba.
¡Qué bien borda! ¡Con qué gracia!
10 Sobre la tela pajiza
ella quisiera bordar
flores de su fantasía.
¡Qué girasol! ¡Qué magnolia
de lentejuelas y cintas!
15 ¡Qué azafranes y qué lunas,
en el mantel de la misa!
Cinco toronjas se endulzan
en la cercana cocina.
Las cinco llagas de Cristo
20 cortadas en Almería.
Por los ojos de la monja
galopan dos caballistas.
Un rumor último y sordo
le despega la camisa,
25 y al mirar nubes y montes
en las yertas lejanías,
se quiebra su corazón
de azúcar y yerbaluisa.
¡Oh, qué llanura empinada

30   con veinte soles arriba!
       ¡Qué ríos puestos de pie
       vislumbra su fantasía!
       Pero sigue con sus flores,
       mientras que de pie, en la brisa,
35   la luz juega el ajedrez
       alto de la celosía.

6

LA CASADA INFIEL

A Lydia Cabrera y a su negrita

Y que yo me la llevé al río
creyendo que era mozuela,
pero tenía marido.

Fue la noche de Santiago
5   y casi por compromiso.
Se apagaron los faroles
y se encendieron los grillos.
En las últimas esquinas
toqué sus pechos dormidos,
10   y se me abrieron de pronto
como ramos de jacintos.
El almidón de su enagua
me sonaba en el oído,
como una pieza de seda
15   rasgada por diez cuchillos.
Sin luz de plata en sus copas
los árboles han crecido
y un horizonte de perros
ladra muy lejos del río.

*

20   Pasadas las zarzamoras,
los juncos y los espinos,
bajo su mata de pelo
hice un hoyo sobre el limo.
Yo me quité la corbata.

25 Ella se quitó el vestido.
    Yo el cinturón con revólver.
    Ella sus cuatro corpiños.
    Ni nardos ni caracolas
    tienen el cutis tan fino,
30 ni los cristales con luna
    relumbran con ese brillo.
    Sus muslos se me escapaban
    como peces sorprendidos,
    la mitad llenos de lumbre,
35 la mitad llenos de frío.
    Aquella noche corrí
    el mejor de los caminos,
    montado en potra de nácar
    sin bridas y sin estribos.
40 No quiero decir, por hombre,
    las cosas que ella me dijo.
    La luz del entendimiento
    me hace ser muy comedido.
    Sucia de besos y arena
45 yo me la llevé del río.
    Con el aire se batían
    las espadas de los lirios.

        Me porté como quien soy.
    Como un gitano legítimo.
50 La regalé un costurero
    grande, de raso pajizo,
    y no quise enamorarme
    porque teniendo marido
    me dijo que era mozuela
55 cuando la llevaba al río.

7

ROMANCE DE LA PENA NEGRA

A José Navarro Pardo

    Las piquetas de los gallos
cavan buscando la aurora,
cuando por el monte oscuro
baja Soledad Montoya.
5   Cobre amarillo su carne,
huele a caballo y a sombra.
Yunques ahumados sus pechos,
gimen canciones redondas.
    —Soledad: ¿por quién preguntas
10 sin compaña y a estas horas?
    —Pregunte por quien pregunte,
dime: ¿a ti qué se te importa?
Vengo a buscar lo que busco,
mi alegría y mi persona.
15 —Soledad de mis pesares,
caballo que se desboca,
al fin encuentra la mar
y se lo tragan las olas.
    —No me recuerdes el mar
20 que la pena negra, brota
en las tierras de aceituna
bajo el rumor de las hojas.
    —¡Soledad, qué pena tienes!
¡Qué pena tan lastimosa!
25 Lloras zumo de limón
agrio de espera y de boca.
    —¡Qué pena tan grande!
Corro mi casa como una loca,

mis dos trenzas por el suelo
30 de la cocina a la alcoba.
¡Qué pena! Me estoy poniendo
de azabache, carne y ropa.
¡Ay mis camisas de hilo!
¡Ay mis muslos de amapola!
35 —Soledad: lava tu cuerpo
con agua de las alondras,
y deja tu corazón
en paz, Soledad Montoya.

*

Por abajo canta el río:
40 volante de cielo y hojas.
Con flores de calabaza
la nueva luz se corona.
¡Oh pena de los gitanos!
Pena limpia y siempre sola.
45 ¡Oh pena de cauce oculto
y madrugada remota!

8
SAN MIGUEL
(GRANADA)

A Diego Buigas de Dalmáu

Se ven desde las barandas,
por el monte, monte, monte,
mulos y sombras de mulos
cargados de girasoles.

5   Sus ojos en las umbrías
se empañan de inmensa noche.
En los recodos del aire
cruje la aurora salobre.

Un cielo de mulos blancos
10 cierra sus ojos de azogue,
dando a la quieta penumbra
un final de corazones.
Y el agua se pone fría
para que nadie la toque.
15 Agua loca y descubierta
por el monte, monte, monte.

*

San Miguel, lleno de encajes
en la alcoba de su torre,
enseña sus bellos muslos
20 ceñidos por los faroles.

Arcángel domesticado
en el gesto de las doce,

finge una cólera dulce
de plumas y ruiseñores.
25   San Miguel canta en los vidrios,
efebo de tres mil noches,
fragante de agua colonia
y lejano de las flores.

*

El mar baila por la playa
30   un poema de balcones.
Las orillas de la luna
pierden juncos, ganan voces.
Vienen manolas comiendo
semillas de girasoles,
35   los culos grandes y ocultos
como planetas de cobre.
Vienen altos caballeros
y damas de triste porte,
morenas por la nostalgia
40   de un ayer de ruiseñores.
Y el obispo de Manila,
ciego de azafrán y pobre,
dice misa con dos filos
para mujeres y hombres.

*

45   San Miguel se estaba quieto
en la alcoba de su torre,
con las enaguas cuajadas
de espejitos y entredoses.

San Miguel, rey de los globos
50   y de los números nones,
en el primor berberisco
de gritos y miradores.

9

SAN RAFAEL
(CORDOBA)

A Juan Izquierdo Croselles

    Coches cerrados llegaban
a las orillas de juncos
donde las ondas alisan
romano torso desnudo.
5 Coches que el Guadalquivir
tiende en su cristal maduro,
entre láminas de flores
y resonancias de nublos.
Los niños tejen y cantan
10 el desengaño del mundo
cerca de los viejos coches
perdidos en el nocturno.
Pero Córdoba no tiembla
bajo el misterio confuso,
15 pues si la sombra levanta
la arquitectura del humo,
un pie de mármol afirma
su casto fulgor enjuto.
Pétalos de lata débil
20 recaman los grises puros
de la brisa, desplegada
sobre los arcos de triunfo.
Y mientras el puente sopla
diez rumores de Neptuno,
25 vendedores de tabaco
huyen por el roto muro.

II

Un solo pez en el agua
que a las dos Córdobas junta.
Blanda Córdoba de juncos.
30 Córdoba de arquitectura.
Niños de cara impasible
en la orilla se desnudan,
aprendices de Tobías
y Merlines de cintura,
35 para fastidiar al pez
en irónica pregunta
si quiere flores de vino
o saltos de media luna.
Pero el pez que dora el agua
40 y los mármoles enluta,
les da lección y equilibrio
de solitaria columna.
El Arcángel aljamiado
de lentejuelas oscuras,
45 en el mitin de las ondas
buscaba rumor y cuna.

*

Un solo pez en el agua.
Dos Córdobas de hermosura.
Córdoba quebrada en chorros.
50 Celeste Córdoba enjuta.

10
SAN GABRIEL
(SEVILLA)

A D. Agustín Viñuales

    Un bello niño de junco,
anchos hombros, fino talle,
piel de nocturna manzana,
boca triste y ojos grandes,
5 nervio de plata caliente,
ronda la desierta calle.
Sus zapatos de charol
rompen las dalias del aire,
con los dos ritmos que cantan
10 breves lutos celestiales.
En la ribera del mar
no hay palma que se le iguale,
ni emperador coronado,
ni lucero caminante.
15 Cuando la cabeza inclina
sobre su pecho de jaspe,
la noche busca llanuras
porque quiere arrodillarse.
Las guitarras suenan solas
20 para San Gabriel Arcángel,
domador de palomillas
y enemigo de los sauces.
—San Gabriel: el niño llora
en el vientre de su madre.
25 No olvides que los gitanos
te regalaron el traje.

II

    Anunciación de los Reyes,
bien lunada y mal vestida,
abre la puerta al lucero
30 que por la calle venía.
El Arcángel San Gabriel,
entre azucena y sonrisa,
biznieto de la Giralda,
se acercaba de visita.
35 En su chaleco bordado
grillos ocultos palpitan.
Las estrellas de la noche
se volvieron campanillas.
—San Gabriel: aquí me tienes
40 con tres clavos de alegría.
Tu fulgor abre jazmines
sobre mi cara encendida.
—Dios te salve, Anunciación.
Morena de maravilla.
45 Tendrás un niño más bello
que los tallos de la brisa.
—¡Ay San Gabriel de mis ojos!
¡Gabrielillo de mi vida!
Para sentarte yo sueño
50 un sillón de clavellinas.
—Dios te salve, Anunciación,
bien lunada y mal vestida.
Tu niño tendrá en el pecho
un lunar y tres heridas.
55 —¡Ay San Gabriel que reluces!
¡Gabrielillo de mi vida!
En el fondo de mis pechos
ya nace la leche tibia.
—Dios te salve, Anunciación.

60   Madre de cien dinastías.
        Aridos lucen tus ojos,
        paisajes de caballista.

                    *

        El niño canta en el seno
        de Anunciación sorprendida.
65   Tres balas de almendra verde
        tiemblan en su vocecita.

        Ya San Gabriel en el aire
        por una escala subía.
        Las estrellas de la noche
70   se volvieron siemprevivas.

11

PRENDIMIENTO DE ANTOÑITO EL CAMBORIO EN EL CAMINO DE SEVILLA

A Margarita Xirgu

Antonio Torres Heredia,
hijo y nieto de Camborios,
con una vara de mimbre
va a Sevilla a ver los toros.
5 Moreno de verde luna,
anda despacio y garboso.
Sus empavonados bucles
le brillan entre los ojos.
A la mitad del camino
10 cortó limones redondos,
y los fue tirando al agua
hasta que la puso de oro.
Y a la mitad del camino,
bajo las ramas de un olmo,
15 Guardia Civil caminera
lo llevó codo con codo.

*

El día se va despacio,
la tarde colgada a un hombro,
dando una larga torera
20 sobre el mar y los arroyos.
Las aceitunas aguardan
la noche de Capricornio,
y una corta brisa, ecuestre,

salta los montes de plomo.
25 Antonio Torres Heredia,
hijo y nieto de Camborios,
viene sin vara de mimbre
entre los cinco tricornios.

—Antonio, ¿quién eres tú?
30 Si te llamaras Camborio,
hubieras hecho una fuente
de sangre con cinco chorros.
Ni tú eres hijo de nadie,
ni legítimo Camborio.
35 ¡Se acabaron los gitanos
que iban por el monte solos!
Están los viejos cuchillos
tiritando bajo el polvo.

*

A las nueve de la noche
40 lo llevan al calabozo,
mientras los guardias civiles
beben limonada todos.
Y a las nueve de la noche
le cierran el calabozo,
45 mientras el cielo reluce
como la grupa de un potro.

12
MUERTE DE ANTOÑITO
EL CAMBORIO

A José Antonio Rubio Sacristán

    Voces de muerte sonaron
cerca del Guadalquivir.
Voces antiguas que cercan
voz de clavel varonil.
5   Les clavó sobre las botas
mordiscos de jabalí.
En la lucha daba saltos
jabonados de delfín.
Bañó con sangre enemiga
10 su corbata carmesí,
pero eran cuatro puñales
y tuvo que sucumbir.
Cuando las estrellas clavan
rejones al agua gris,
15 cuando los erales sueñan
verónicas de alhelí,
voces de muerte sonaron
cerca del Guadalquivir.

       *

    —Antonio Torres Heredia,
20 Camborio de dura crin,
moreno de verde luna,
voz de clavel varonil:
¿quién te ha quitado la vida
cerca del Guadalquivir?

25 —Mis cuatro primos Heredias
   hijos de Benamejí.
   Lo que en otros no envidiaban,
   ya lo envidiaban en mí.
   Zapatos color corinto,
30 medallones de marfil,
   y este cutis amasado
   con aceituna y jazmín.
   —¡Ay Antoñito el Camborio
   digno de una Emperatriz!
35 Acuérdate de la Virgen
   porque te vas a morir.
   —¡Ay Federico García,
   llama a la Guardia Civil!
   Ya mi talle se ha quebrado
40 como caña de maíz.

*

   Tres golpes de sangre tuvo
   y se murió de perfil.
   Viva moneda que nunca
   se volverá a repetir.
45 Un ángel marchoso pone
   su cabeza en un cojín.
   Otros de rubor cansado
   encendieron un candil.
   Y cuando los cuatro primos
50 llegan a Benamejí,
   voces de muerte cesaron
   cerca del Guadalquivir.

13

MUERTO DE AMOR

A Margarita Manso

—¿Qué es aquello que reluce
por los altos corredores?
—Cierra la puerta, hijo mío,
acaban de dar las once.
5   —En mis ojos, sin querer,
relumbran cuatro faroles.
—Será que la gente aquella
estará fregando el cobre.

*

Ajo de agónica plata
10   la luna menguante, pone
cabelleras amarillas
a las amarillas torres.
La noche llama temblando
al cristal de los balcones
15   perseguida por los mil
perros que no la conocen,
y un olor de vino y ámbar
viene de los corredores.

*

Brisas de caña mojada
20   y rumor de viejas voces
resonaban por el arco
roto de la media noche.

Bueyes y rosas dormían.
Sólo por los corredores
25 las cuatro luces clamaban
con el furor de San Jorge.
Tristes mujeres del valle
bajaban su sangre de hombre,
tranquila de flor cortada
30 y amarga de muslo joven.
Viejas mujeres del río
lloraban al pie del monte,
un minuto intransitable
de cabelleras y nombres.
35 Fachadas de cal, ponían
cuadrada y blanca la noche.
Serafines y gitanos
tocaban acordeones.
—Madre, cuando yo me muera
40 que se enteren los señores.
Pon telegramas azules
que vayan del Sur al Norte.
    Siete gritos, siete sangres,
siete adormideras dobles
45 quebraron opacas lunas
en los oscuros salones.
Lleno de manos cortadas
y coronitas de flores,
el mar de los juramentos
50 resonaba, no sé dónde.
Y el cielo daba portazos
al brusco rumor del bosque,
mientras clamaban las luces
en los altos corredores.

14
ROMANCE DEL EMPLAZADO

Para Emilio Aladrén

¡Mi soledad sin descanso!
Ojos chicos de mi cuerpo
y grandes de mi caballo,
no se cierran por la noche
5   ni miran al otro lado
donde se aleja tranquilo
un sueño de trece barcos.
Sino que limpios y duros
escuderos desvelados,
10 mis ojos miran un norte
de metales y peñascos
donde mi cuerpo sin venas
consulta naipes helados.

*

Los densos bueyes del agua
15 embisten a los muchachos
que se bañan en las lunas
de sus cuernos ondulados.
Y los martillos cantaban
sobre los yunques sonámbulos
20 el insomnio del jinete
y el insomnio del caballo.

*

El veinticinco de junio
le dijeron a el Amargo:

—Ya puedes cortar, si gustas,
25   las adelfas de tu patio.
Pinta una cruz en la puerta
y pon tu nombre debajo,
porque cicutas y ortigas
nacerán en tu costado,
30   y agujas de cal mojada
te morderán los zapatos.
Será de noche, en lo oscuro,
por los montes imantados
donde los bueyes del agua
35   beben los juncos soñando.
Pide luces y campanas.
Aprende a cruzar las manos,
y gusta los aires fríos
de metales y peñascos.
40   Porque dentro de dos meses
yacerás amortajado.

*

Espadón de nebulosa
mueve en el aire Santiago.
Grave silencio, de espalda,
45   manaba el cielo combado.

*

El veinticinco de junio
abrió sus ojos Amargo,
y el veinticinco de agosto
se tendió para cerrarlos.
50   Hombres bajaban la calle
para ver al emplazado,
que fijaba sobre el muro
su soledad con descanso.

Y la sábana impecable,
55 de duro acento romano,
daba equilibrio a la muerte
con las rectas de sus paños.

15
ROMANCE DE LA GUARDIA CIVIL ESPAÑOLA

A Juan Guerrero
Cónsul general de la poesía

Los caballos negros son.
Las herraduras son negras.
Sobre las capas relucen
manchas de tinta y de cera.
5 Tienen, por eso no lloran,
de plomo las calaveras.
Con el alma de charol
vienen por la carretera.
Jorobados y nocturnos,
10 por donde animan ordenan
silencios de goma oscura
y miedos de fina arena.
Pasan, si quieren pasar,
y ocultan en la cabeza
15 una vaga astronomía
de pistolas inconcretas.

*

¡Oh ciudad de los gitanos!
En las esquinas banderas.
La luna y la calabaza
20 con las guindas en conserva.
¡Oh ciudad de los gitanos!
¿Quién te vio y no te recuerda?

Ciudad de dolor y almizcle,
con las torres de canela.

*

25   Cuando llegaba la noche,
noche que noche nochera,
los gitanos en sus fraguas
forjaban soles y flechas.
Un caballo malherido
30   llamaba a todas las puertas.
Gallos de vidrio cantaban
por Jerez de la Frontera.
El viento, vuelve desnudo
la esquina de la sorpresa,
35   en la noche platinoche,
noche que noche nochera.

*

La Virgen y San José
perdieron sus castañuelas,
y buscan a los gitanos
40   para ver si las encuentran.
La Virgen viene vestida
con un traje de alcaldesa
de papel de chocolate
con los collares de almendras.
45   San José mueve los brazos
bajo una capa de seda.
Detrás va Pedro Domecq
con tres sultanes de Persia.
La media luna, soñaba
50   un éxtasis de cigüeña.
Estandartes y faroles

invaden las azoteas.
Por los espejos sollozan
bailarinas sin caderas.
55 Agua y sombra, sombra y agua
por Jerez de la Frontera.

*

¡Oh ciudad de los gitanos!
En las esquinas banderas.
Apaga tus verdes luces
60 que viene la benemérita.
¡Oh ciudad de los gitanos!
¿Quién te vio y no te recuerda?
Dejadla lejos del mar
sin peines para sus crenchas.

*

65 Avanzan de dos en fondo
a la ciudad de la fiesta.
Un rumor de siemprevivas
invade las cartucheras.
Avanzan de dos en fondo.
70 Doble nocturno de tela.
El cielo, se les antoja,
una vitrina de espuelas.

*

La ciudad, libre de miedo,
multiplicaba sus puertas.
75 Cuarenta guardias civiles
entran a saco por ellas.
Los relojes se pararon,
y el coñac de las botellas

se disfrazó de noviembre
80 para no infundir sospechas.
Un vuelo de gritos largos
se levantó en las veletas.
Los sables cortan las brisas
que los cascos atropellan.
85 Por las calles de penumbra
huyen las gitanas viejas
con los caballos dormidos
y las orzas de monedas.
Por las calles empinadas
90 suben las capas siniestras,
dejando detrás fugaces
remolinos de tijeras.

En el Portal de Belén
los gitanos se congregan.
95 San José, lleno de heridas,
amortaja a una doncella.
Tercos fusiles agudos
por toda la noche suenan.
La Virgen cura a los niños
100 con salivilla de estrella.
Pero la Guardia Civil
avanza sembrando hogueras,
donde joven y desnuda
la imaginación se quema.
105 Rosa la de los Camborios
gime sentada en su puerta
con sus dos pechos cortados
puestos en una bandeja.
Y otras muchachas corrían
110 perseguidas por sus trenzas,
en un aire donde estallan
rosas de pólvora negra.
Cuando todos los tejados

eran surcos en la tierra,
115 el alba meció sus hombros
en largo perfil de piedra.

*

¡Oh ciudad de los gitanos!
La Guardia Civil se aleja
por un túnel de silencio
120 mientras las llamas te cercan.

¡Oh ciudad de los gitanos!
¿Quién te vio y no te recuerda?
Que te busquen en mi frente.
Juego de luna y arena.

TRES ROMANCES HISTORICOS

16
MARTIRIO DE SANTA OLALLA

A Rafael Martínez Nadal

I

PANORAMA DE MÉRIDA

    Por la calle brinca y corre
caballo de larga cola,
mientras juegan o dormitan
viejos soldados de Roma.
5 Medio monte de Minervas
abre sus brazos sin hojas.
Agua en vilo redoraba
las aristas de las rocas.
Noche de torsos yacentes
10 y estrellas de nariz rota
aguarda grietas del alba
para derrumbarse toda.
De cuando en cuando sonaban
blasfemias de cresta roja.
15 Al gemir la santa niña,
quiebra el cristal de las copas.
La rueda afila cuchillos
y garfios de aguda comba.
Brama el toro de los yunques,
20 y Mérida se corona
de nardos casi despiertos
y tallos de zarzamora.

II

EL MARTIRIO

Flora desnuda se sube
por escalerillas de agua.
25 El Cónsul pide bandeja
para los senos de Olalla.
Un chorro de venas verdes
le brota de la garganta.
Su sexo tiembla enredado
30 como un pájaro en las zarzas.
Por el suelo, ya sin norma,
brincan sus manos cortadas
que aún pueden cruzarse en tenue
oración decapitada.
35 Por los rojos agujeros
donde sus pechos estaban
se ven cielos diminutos
y arroyos de leche blanca.
Mil arbolillos de sangre
40 le cubren toda la espalda
y oponen húmedos troncos
al bisturí de las llamas.
Centuriones amarillos
de carne gris, desvelada,
45 llegan al cielo sonando
sus armaduras de plata.
Y mientras vibra confusa
pasión de crines y espadas,
el Cónsul porta en bandeja
50 senos ahumados de Olalla.

III

INFIERNO Y GLORIA

Nieve ondulada reposa.
Olalla pende del árbol.
Su desnudo de carbón
tizna los aires helados.
55 Noche tirante reluce.
Olalla muerta en el árbol.
Tinteros de las ciudades
vuelcan la tinta despacio.
Negros maniquís de sastre
60 cubren la nieve del campo
en largas filas que gimen
su silencio mutilado.
Nieve partida comienza.
Olalla blanca en el árbol.
65 Escuadras de níquel juntan
los picos en su costado.

*

Una Custodia reluce
sobre los cielos quemados,
entre gargantas de arroyo
70 y ruiseñores en ramos.
¡Saltan vidrios de colores!
Olalla blanca en lo blanco.
Angeles y serafines
dicen: Santo, Santo, Santo.

17

BURLA DE DON PEDRO A CABALLO
ROMANCE CON LAGUNAS

A Jean Cassou

Por una vereda
venía Don Pedro.
¡Ay cómo lloraba
el caballero!
5 Montado en un ágil
caballo sin freno,
venía en la busca
del pan y del beso.
Todas las ventanas
10 preguntan al viento
por el llanto oscuro
del caballero.

PRIMERA LAGUNA

Bajo el agua
siguen las palabras.
15 Sobre el agua
una luna redonda
se baña,
dando envidia a la otra
¡tan alta!
20 En la orilla,
un niño
ve las lunas y dice:
¡Noche; toca los platillos!

SIGUE

A una ciudad lejana
25 ha llegado Don Pedro.
Una ciudad de oro
entre un bosque de cedros.
¿Es Belén? Por el aire
yerbaluisa y romero.
30 Brillan las azoteas
y las nubes. Don Pedro
pasa por arcos rotos.
Dos mujeres y un viejo
con velones de plata
35 le salen al encuentro.
Los chopos dicen: No.
Y el ruiseñor: Veremos.

SEGUNDA LAGUNA

Bajo el agua
siguen las palabras.
40 Sobre el peinado del agua
un círculo de pájaros y llamas.
Y por los cañaverales,
testigos que conocen lo que falta.
Sueño concreto y sin norte
45 de madera de guitarra.

SIGUE

Por el camino llano
dos mujeres y un viejo
con velones de plata
van al cementerio.
50 Entre los azafranes

han encontrado muerto
el sombrío caballo
de Don Pedro.
Voz secreta de tarde
55 balaba por el cielo.
Unicornio de ausencia
rompe en cristal su cuerno.
La gran ciudad lejana
está ardiendo
60 y un hombre va llorando
tierras adentro.
Al Norte hay una estrella.
Al Sur un marinero.

ÚLTIMA LAGUNA

Bajo el agua
65 están las palabras.
Limo de voces perdidas.
Sobre la flor enfriada
está Don Pedro olvidado
¡ay! jugando con las ranas.

18

THAMAR Y AMNON

Para Alfonso García Valdecasas

La luna gira en el cielo
sobre las tierras sin agua
mientras el verano siembra
rumores de tigre y llama.
5 Por encima de los techos
nervios de metal sonaban.
Aire rizado venía
con los balidos de lana.
La tierra se ofrece llena
10 de heridas cicatrizadas,
o estremecida de agudos
cauterios de luces blancas.

*

Thamar estaba soñando
pájaros en su garganta,
15 al son de panderos fríos
y cítaras enlunadas.
Su desnudo en el alero,
agudo norte de palma,
pide copos a su vientre
20 y granizo a sus espaldas.
Thamar estaba cantando
desnuda por la terraza.
Alrededor de sus pies,
cinco palomas heladas.
25 Amnón, delgado y concreto,

en la torre la miraba,
llenas las ingles de espuma
y oscilaciones la barba.
Su desnudo iluminado
30   se tendía en la terraza,
con un rumor entre dientes
de flecha recién clavada.
Amnón estaba mirando
la luna redonda y baja,
35   y vio en la luna los pechos
durísimos de su hermana.

*

Amnón a las tres y media
se tendió sobre la cama.
Toda la alcoba sufría
40   con sus ojos llenos de alas.
La luz maciza, sepulta
pueblos en la arena parda,
o descubre transitorio
coral de rosas y dalias.
45   Linfa de pozo oprimida
brota silencio en las jarras.
En el musgo de los troncos
la cobra tendida canta.
Amnón gime por la tela
50   fresquísima de la cama.
Yedra del escalofrío
cubre su carne quemada.
Thamar entró silenciosa
en la alcoba silenciada,
55   color de vena y Danubio,
turbia de huellas lejanas.
—Thamar, bórrame los ojos
con tu fija madrugada.

Mis hilos de sangre tejen
60 volantes sobre tu falda.
—Déjame tranquila, hermano.
Son tus besos en mi espalda
avispas y vientecillos
en doble enjambre de flautas.
65 —Thamar, en tus pechos altos
hay dos peces que me llaman
y en las yemas de tus dedos
rumor de rosa encerrada.

*

Los cien caballos del rey
70 en el patio relinchaban.
Sol en cubos resistía
la delgadez de la parra.
Ya la coge del cabello,
ya la camisa le rasga.
75 Corales tibios dibujan
arroyos en rubio mapa.

*

¡Oh, qué gritos se sentían
por encima de las casas!
Qué espesura de puñales
80 y túnicas desgarradas.
Por las escaleras tristes
esclavos suben y bajan.
Embolos y muslos juegan
bajo las nubes paradas.
85 Alrededor de Thamar
gritan vírgenes gitanas
y otras recogen las gotas
de su flor martirizada.

      Paños blancos, enrojecen
90 en las alcobas cerradas.
      Rumores de tibia aurora
      pámpanos y peces cambian.

           *

      Violador enfurecido,
      Amnón huye con su jaca.
95 Negros le dirigen flechas
      en los muros y atalayas.
      Y cuando los cuatro cascos
      eran cuatro resonancias,
      David con unas tijeras
100 cortó las cuerdas del arpa.

ENDNOTES

In the notes that follow I extract from my book of commentaries the information most likely to be helpful to the first-time reader of *Romancero gitano* and supplement it with guidance on linguistic difficulties. Inevitably there is much overlapping, especially where the difficulty of a poem lies less in its language than in its overall progression. Given the combination of limited space and practical aim I do not indicate pre-*RG* variants except in a few cases where they throw light on the definitive text. On six points where published *RG* editions differ in other than punctuation, typography or printing error I append a note.

1. ROMANCE DE LA LUNA, LUNA

The moon comes down to the gypsy forge, binds the child with her spell-like dance and finally leads him away across the sky. It is an invented myth, said Lorca: 'La luna como bailarina mortal [. . .]. Mito de la luna sobre tierras de danza dramática, Andalucía interior concentrada y religiosa' (III, 342). In fact tradition and invention are characteristically fused: on the one hand there is an echo of popular superstition, for the moon is reputed to carry away children who look at it too much, and behind this, a wider, primitive awareness of the moon as an influence on human destinies and a bringer of death; on the other hand there is Lorca's own invention, with the moon presented, appropriately in an Andalusian gypsy context, as a seductive dancer. In short, with fusion of the two: 'la luna como bailarina mortal'. The emphasis throughout is on the interplay of seductiveness and detachment; in Lorca's own words (from an early draft of the poem), 'baile de amor y frío'.

    2. *with her bustle of nards.* White flowers appropriate to the dress of the anthropomorphic moon, but also with a suggestion of inaccessibility that will be developed throughout the poem.

    7. *lúbrica.* A learned word of complex meaning (cf. English *lubricious*) suggesting sinuous, almost snake-like fascination and seduction.

18. *sentir* for *oír*; frequent in Andalusia.

20. *my starched whiteness*. The dress again, white and unyielding (compare the *senos de duro estaño*, shining and without warmth, and the moon's heart, appropriate for making white rings and necklaces).

22. *beating the drum of the plain*, with sound imagery to produce the effect of a galloping horse.

26–8. As with the moon, physical and psychological characteristics are superimposed: *bronze* (swarthy complexion and noble profile; cf. *cabezas levantadas*) and *eyes half-closed* (oriental gypsy eyes suggestive of dreamlike qualities; cf. *sueño*).

Note especially, throughout the poem, the magical, incantatory effect of repeated sounds and words and of variations on repetition (e.g. lines 3–4, 9, 13/19, 17, 29–30, 35–6).

2. PRECIOSA Y EL AIRE

The first poem, said Lorca, was a myth of inland Andalusia; this one is a myth of coastal Andalusia, 'mito de playa tartesa donde el aire es suave como pelusa de melocotón y donde todo drama o danza está sostenido por una aguja inteligente de burla o de ironía' (III, 342). It tells of the wind's pursuit of a young gypsy girl and of her narrow escape. As in 'Romance de la luna, luna', then, a vulnerable human being is beset by a personified force of nature. Like the moon the anthropomorphic pursuing wind has its origins in popular culture; so does the female object of pursuit. But Preciosa has a more specific and immediate literary source too: Cervantes's Preciosa, the formidably virtuous protagonist of his exemplary novel *La gitanilla*. In imagery too there are notable echoes of Cervantes's work.

1. *her parchment moon*. Her tambourine (cf. 29), which shows up white against the surrounding darkness and, together with *aire* in the title, suggests a significant relationship with the previous poem.

3. *amphibious*. Because the path is partly dry and partly under water (cf. *cristales y laureles*, 4).

13–16. The *gitanos del agua* have been variously interpreted as real-life gypsies, fish and sea-waves. More probably this is a visionary image of sprite-like figures who, in their sheer joy of creation, are likened to the gypsies — and contrasted to the solid, utilitarian English: on the one hand, *glorietas de caracolas / y ramos de pino verde*; on the other, *blancas torres* appropriately guarded by the forces of law and order.

Caracolas are usually *seashells* but in Granada refer also to a specific climbing plant. Suggested translation: *arbours of shell-flowers*. The line *y ramos de pino verde* appears frequently in traditional songs, often associated with the Nativity.

21. In Spanish popular tradition Saint Christopher (*Cristóbal*) is seen as a hefty, rugged, muscular being. He is thus an appropriate image of the wind which, in *cante jondo*, 'aparece como un gigante preocupado de derribar estrellas y disparar nebulosas' (III, 209). Lorca here increases the effect by using the augmentative *Cristobalón* (cf. later, *el viento-hombrón, the big-man wind*). It is of course ironic that Saint Christopher is also the patron saint of travellers.

23–4. The subject of *tocando*, it is said, is Saint Christopher, who naturally plays a wind instrument. In view of *dulce* and *ausente* one might prefer to see Preciosa as the subject. She would thus be beating her tambourine and at the same time imitating softly to herself the sound of an accompanying pipe (surely not a bagpipe, *gaita gallega*, but the *gaita* proper, a rustic woodwind instrument much used, together with tabor or tambourine, in popular Spanish fiestas). Lines 35–6, where nature takes up the playing, seem to support this suggestion.

33. *The sea scowls its murmur.* Superposition of sound and sight, the waves of the murmuring sea being seen as scowls of disapproval.

38. *or the randy old wind will catch you* (cf. *un viejo verde, a lustful old man, dirty old man*).

40. A common line in *saetas* and other songs of Holy Week to indicate the approaching figure of Christ. One notes, here as elsewhere, Lorca's bringing together of Christian and pagan references. In similar fashion the wind's *lenguas relucientes* (42; cf. 22) seem to echo the Holy Ghost's 'cloven tongues like as of fire' (Acts 2:3).

3. REYERTA

Gypsy quarrels and fights, usually between members of rival families, are commonplace in Andalusia and are much reported in the popular press. At first sight it is tempting to see Lorca's poem as simply the recounting of such an event, with the death of one of the protagonists, the arrival of the examining magistrate and the flight of the survivors. Lorca believed he had expressed something deeper, more mysterious and of wider significance: 'esa lucha sorda latente en Andalucía y en toda España de grupos que se atacan sin saber por qué, por causas misteriosas, por una mirada, por una rosa, porque un hombre de pronto siente un insecto sobre la mejilla, por un amor de hace dos siglos' (III, 343). With his successive changes of title — from 'Reyerta de mozos' (*La Verdad* 59; 10 October 1926) to 'Reyerta de gitanos' (*L'Amic de les Arts* 15; 30 June 1927) to 'Reyerta' (1928) — Lorca was perhaps seeking expression for this belief, with transition from a title suggestive of mere anecdote, through gypsy drama to a potentially mythical 'Reyerta', with attention fully concentrated on the fight itself.

2. *Albacete.* The classic centre of Spanish knife manufacture, especially noted for the *navaja de Albacete* with its characteristically curved and tapered blade (which underlies the image of the angels' wings in 15–16).

3. *beautiful with rival (enemy, opponent's) blood.* The stylised pageantry of bloodshed, akin to the bullfight.

5. *A harsh playing-card light.* A reference to a game of cards has been suggested. Since cards, especially in a gypsy context, are associated with fortune-telling, the harshness of destiny foretold may be more relevant (cf. *agrio verde*, 6). The image was probably prompted by the eleventh card in the Spanish pack which depicts a clearly outlined horse and rider.

11–12. *The bull of strife clambers up the walls.* Like a bull climbing the *barrera* of a bullring. But *subirse por las paredes* is also a popular expression meaning *to go off the deep end, climb up the wall* (in anger or exasperation). In the Introduction I suggest the relevance of Bruegel's painting and point to other echoes of Renaissance painting in lines 9–22: old women who weep *en la copa de un olivo* (9–10), ministering black angels with wings of Albacete clasp knives (13–16), the imagery of wounds (19–20), Juan Antonio's triumphant ride along the highway to death (21–2). By means of neo-primitive stylisation — and a touch of Andalusian *guasa* that anticipates the response of the *juez* (27–30) — Lorca is able both to present the horror of bloodshed and suffering and at the same time to prevent Romantic-type emotional involvement on the part of his reader. It is akin to classical tragedy: harsh action veiled and universalised through lyrical stylisation (cf. the end of *Bodas de sangre*). It is also akin to a duality noted in Poem 1: seduction and detachment, *baile de amor y frío.*

17. *Montilla.* In the province of Cordoba.

25–6. *Slithered blood moans its muted serpent song.* A remarkable image that combines personification, transferred epithet (hypallage), oxymoron, metaphor and onomatopoeia.

29-30. The wars of Romans and Carthaginians for the possession of Spain are well known. What the examining magistrate here means, then, is that it is the same old story: age-old rivalries and conflicts resulting in death.

31-4. Fury and suffering alike would detract from the all-important gypsy profile of bronze and dream. In line 7 the fury of the protagonists was appropriately transferred to their horses; in 31-4 it is the afternoon that expresses their torment, swooning, mad with pain and burning, on their wounded thighs.

35-8. Escaping gypsies? Evening clouds? Or simply, as I believe, black angels? 36. de poniente: *La Verdad* (1926), 1935, 1937, 1938, MH, MGP; de Poniente: *L'Amic de les Arts* (1927); del poniente: 1928, 1929, Ag.

4. ROMANCE SONAMBULO

On the rooftop of her house a girl awaits the return of her lover, apparently away on a smuggling expedition. The lover arrives badly wounded, goes up with the girl's father to where the girl was waiting and finds her dead. Civil guards come to arrest him. This, it seems, is the narrative framework of the poem. But mere narrative plays little part and pointers to a smuggling expedition are glimpsed only momentarily amidst a succession of dreamlike images. 'Hay una gran sensación de anécdota, un agudo ambiente dramático,' commented Lorca, 'y nadie sabe lo que pasa ni aun yo, porque el misterio poético es también misterio para el poeta que lo comunica, pero que muchas veces lo ignora' (III, 341). The poem is a characteristically Lorcan 'sleepwalking ballad' of yearning and lamentation.

1-4. *For it's green that I want you, green. / Green wind. Green branches. / The boat on the sea / and the horse in the mountain.* A magical, incantatory opening to establish an initial plane of longing and illusion: life, freshness and freedom, with everything in its proper place.

5-12. Indications of withdrawal from life suggest a break already with the longed-for illusion of 1-4. Thus — one of several examples — green in line 2 suggested freshness; now, applied to flesh and hair (7), it suggests lunar light and, beyond that, putrefaction (compare the association of moon and death in Poem 1). The world around is more alive than the girl herself (11-12).

13–24. We are reminded of the plane of illusion (13), but it is again condemned, this time by the inhospitable world of nature, with *stars of hoarfrost* (14), *fish of shade* (15), tamed wind (like a domestic animal) rubbed by the *sandpaper* of the *fig tree*'s dry branches (17–18) — all very different from the longed-for *Verde viento. Verdes ramas* — and, as the dawn approaches, the agaves along the mountain top are seen as the *bristling* of a *filching cat* that senses threat (19–20). Even the questions about someone's approach are unanswered (21). Now the girl's waiting seems even more forlorn (22–4) and appropriately echoes a well-known and much glossed traditional poem of unhappy love: 'Miraba la mar / la mal casada, / que miraba la mar / cómo es ancha y larga'. Compare lines 5–7 and 22–4, identifying the common elements and the difference, and consider the effect.

25. *Compadre.* A word much used in Andalusia. Here *friend, pal, buddy*.

30. *the passes of Cabra.* In the south of the province of Cordoba, an area formerly famous for its smugglers and bandits.

38. *with cambric sheets* (i.e. sheets of fine linen). Like the *steel bed* (36–7), part of the gypsy's longed-for illusion as death approaches.

39. ves: 1928–1938, MH; veis: ms (*2*, 1408), Ag, MGP. In support of *ves* attention has been drawn to lines 67–8; in support of *veis*, to 47 and 49. I opt for *ves* because all *RG* editions published in Lorca's lifetime have it. Grammatically and stylistically too it is perhaps preferable, with an effective crescendo effect in the broadening of audience in 47 and 49, so that the reader too feels involved in the gypsy's clamour.

41. Stylisation of wounds (cf. *lirios* and *granada*, 3:19–20).

50–2. *up to the green railings. Handrails of the moon down which the water thunders.* The physical *baranda* has now been transformed into a further image of illusion.

59–60. 'Si me preguntan ustedes por qué digo yo: "Mil panderos de cristal herían la madrugada", les diré que los he visto en manos de ángeles y de árboles, pero no sabré decir más, ni mucho menos explicar su significado' (III, 343). The suggestion is of a procession of suffering under the dawning sky.

73–8. The girl is dead, floating on the surface of the water. The icicle of moonbeam recalls the *luna gitana* (10) and suggests that the moon has bound the girl in her spell, as she did the child in Poem 1, and enticed her finally to the water where she lies. The title, it now seems, refers not only to the dreamlike imagery and atmosphere of the poem but also, more specifically, to the manner of the girl's death.

5. LA MONJA GITANA

The problem of convents, said Lorca in his teenage *Impresiones y paisajes* (1918), is to forget. 'Las monjas, en su debilidad infantil, se encerraron en el convento, tapándose el camino del olvidar. Lo que quieren olvidar lo convierten en presente de su alma' (III, 112). Similarly with men who shut themselves away in monasteries (III, 25). The cloister, Lorca believed, is appropriate only for those who have lost their vitality; for others it is a torment; the greater the vitality, the greater the torment. It is in this context that one notes the title of the present poem: on the one hand the protagonist is a gypsy — freedom, vitality, *gracia*, fantasy —; on the other she is a nun — confinement, discipline, menial tasks. As we see in the course of the poem, she epitomises one of Lorca's most persistent concerns, vitality and its repression. There was something similar in the previous poem, with its emphasis on man's illusion and life's disillusion. As further context for appreciation it is relevant to know that in Andalusia convents are most commonly small and, from outside, scarcely distinguishable from other houses: whitewashed, with small latticed windows behind which perhaps only half a dozen nuns live in seclusion, devoted to prayer, needlework and, in certain cases, the making of confectionery.

1. Cf. 'Me gusta Granada con delirio [...]; vivir cerca de lo que uno ama y siente. Cal, mirto y surtidor' (III, 734).

5–8. *Araña* is usually translated and interpreted as *chandelier*. More probably it is a *cobweb* or *spider's web*, with a relevant suggestion of ensnarement (cf. 'la araña gris del tiempo' which ensnares the poet's heart, I, 27). The *siete pájaros del prisma* are of course the colours of the rainbow as refracted in the web (cf. I, 273). In contrast to the birds' flight the distant growling of the church (perhaps a pointer to the organ, which Lorca disliked, III, 892–3) suggests a bear-like hug of death (cf. I, 478).

13–16. The colourful flowers that she would *like* to embroider — instead of the more modest *gillyflowers* (3).

17–20. The smell of pungent grapefruits from the kitchen reflects the bitterness of the nun's own situation and prompts recollection of the traditional five wounds of Christ, causing the grapefruits also to be imagined as five. The sweetening grapefruits recall a traditional occupation of nuns in Andalusia, the making of crystallised fruits.

21-4. '¿dos [caballistas], o uno, reflejado en cada ojo, ya que Lorca dice *por los ojos de la monja* y no *por el campo*?' (González Muela). As the sound of galloping fades into the distance, a tremor runs through the nun (cf. an earlier draft: *Y siente por sus espaldas / un negro chorro de hormigas*), making her aware of her habit as something separate from herself and thus as an element of confinement and repression.

29-32. Her longing continues, now for a steep plain and for rivers on foot.

33-6. Back to the reality of lines 3-4, while the light, alone on foot, casts taunting shadows of the lattice high up on the wall of the cell. The gypsy nun did not *see* the horsemen, then. Prompted by the sound, she projected their image from within. Hence her longing for a steep plain and rivers on foot: so that she could see them from her cell instead of the mere *yertas lejanías* of clouds and mountains.

Even more clearly than others this poem illustrates Lorca's expressionism, with the creation of settings that reflect the emotive state of the protagonist.

6. LA CASADA INFIEL

A gypsy recounts a sexual adventure with a married woman. It is Lorca's best known and most quoted poem. Despite initial enthusiasm and continued recitation of the poem to friends Lorca described it in his lecture-reading as 'gracioso de forma y de imagen' but 'pura anécdota andaluza'. He continued: 'Es popular hasta la desesperación, y como lo considero lo más primario, lo más halagador de sensualidades y lo menos andaluz, no lo leo' (III, 343). It is nevertheless an extremely fine poem and it reveals some of the best qualities of his writing. Of all the poems in the book it is the one in which Lorca himself is most clearly not the narrator.

1-3. According to Lorca's brother the poet heard the opening three lines recited by a muleteer during a journey that the brothers made together through the Sierra Nevada, though Lorca himself later had no recollection of this and continued to believe that the lines were his own creation. I have myself collectd the following *bulería* (relevant to lines 1-2 and 22-3) from Andalusian oral tradition:

Que yo no me la llevé a la playa,
que ella se vino conmigo.
Y por cabecera la puse
la cola de una caballa [a tunny-like fish].

Mozuela refers in Andalusian usage to an unmarried girl.

4. Appropriately the night of Saint James (25 July), Spain's patron saint.

6–7. Hard imagery and synaesthesia (lights that go out and crickets that light up) to mark the transition from town to country, civilisation to nature, with emphasis on senses in the lines that follow.

15. A pointer of course to the gypsy's clawing fingernails. But beware of diluting the impact of the evoked plane by mere substitution.

16–19. As in the previous poem the setting is described from the viewpoint of the protagonists. Since they are now among the trees, down by the river, the trees seem to have grown and are no longer seen with moonlight on them. Distant barking creates a horizon of sound (further synaesthesia).

24–7. Notice the humorous, character-revealing contrast in the gypsy's account: between his own modest undressing and the girl's eager stripping-down.

28. Cf. 2:15

33, 36–9. The sexual act is appropriately presented in terms of gypsy activities, poaching and riding.

40–3. Further humour in the gypsy's proclaimed discretion (with notably discordant *entendimiento* and *comedido*), especially after what he has already revealed — and not merely about what the girl said.

49. *like a purebred gypsy, like a gypsy through and through.*

50. La regalé: 1928–37, Ag; Le regalé: ms (*A* I, 148), *RO* (1928), 1938, MH, MGP. I opt for the traditional text with *laísmo*. Against *La* one can argue (1) that the manuscript and first published version have *Le* and (2) that *laísmo* is not characteristic of Andalusian linguistic usage; for it one can argue (1) that *La* appeared in all editions of *RG* published in Lorca's lifetime, including some at least that he revised, (2) that Lorca uses *laísmo* elsewhere in his writings (II, 468) and (3) that *laísmo*, with its suggestion — throughout Spain — of *chulo* swagger, is psychologically relevant to the gypsy protagonist of this poem (cf. his repeated *yoísmo*, 1, 24, 26, 45) and therefore, presumably, the result of deliberate revision for publication — and republication — in book form. Despite the general non-*laísmo* of Andalusian usage one notes similarly relevant *laísmo* in the *bulería* quoted earlier — from an Andalusian informant.

7. ROMANCE DE LA PENA NEGRA

This is one of the finest poems in the book and the one that most closely captures the dark passion and fatalism of Andalusian *cante jondo*. In 1922 Lorca was involved in the organisation of the famous *cante jondo* festival in Granada and both then and later he lectured enthusiastically on the art of *cante*. 'No hay nada, absolutamente nada, igual en toda España, ni en estilización, ni en ambiente, ni en justeza emocional,' he declared. He emphasised also *cante*'s basic concern with love and death, the 'terrible pregunta que no tiene contestación', the pathos, the absence of half tone, the night setting, the close identification of woman and *pena* .... The transition to his later comments on 'Romance de la pena negra' is easily made:

> La Pena de Soledad Montoya es la raíz del pueblo andaluz. No es angustia porque con pena se puede sonreír, ni es un dolor que ciega puesto que jamás produce llanto; es un ansia sin objeto, es un amor agudo a nada, con una seguridad de que la muerte (preocupación perenne de Andalucía) está respirando detrás de la puerta (III, 344).

Soledad Montoya's *pena*, then, is the same *pena* that finds expression in *cante jondo*. It tells of the sorrow of a people but, like *cante*, reveals itself 'con los acentos de un duelo personal e íntimo' (Rafael Cansinos Assens, *La copla andaluza* [1933], Madrid 1976, p. 29).

1–2. *The picks of the roosters are digging in search of the dawn.* Cockcrows (sound) are presented as digging (sight). Note the dual emphasis on attempted escape from darkness, in the cocks and in Soledad Montoya.

5–8. Pointers to gypsy appearance and gypsy occupations, but with more sombre resonances too. Note the anvils, which suggest beating of the breasts, and the transferred epithet, with *redondas* (of breasts) applied to the wailed songs.

15. *Soledad of my sorrows.* Formed on the model of expressions of endearment such as *Felipe de mi alma, Mari-Pepa de mi vida, Madre de mi corazón*.

16–18. A basic notion in Lorca: to give way to one's passion leads to death (with *encuentra la mar* as a threatening solution of the quest indicated in lines 2, 9, 11, 13).

29. *my two braids* (*tresses, plaits*) *trailing the floor*.

31–4. Step by step Soledad has become identified with the *pena negra* of *cante jondo*, to the point, now, that body and clothes have taken on its blackness. 'La mujer, en el cante jondo, se llama Pena,' said Lorca (III, 209).

35–8. The narrator's prescription for cure, appropriately in terms of gypsy magic, with a suggestion of dawn and morning dew (by association with the larks).

39–42. A shift from the pathos of dark mountain and tormented Soledad to the delight of dawn, with the leaf-spangled river that skirts the mountain seen as the *flounce* of a dress and the colour of the morning sky as a crown of *pumpkin flowers*. The dawn that the cocks were digging for in the opening lines has come. But echoes of the colloquial expression *dar calabazas* (*to cold-shoulder* [*a lover*], *send packing, reject, spurn*) suggest that for Soledad the earlier pointers to abandonment and bitter waiting are still unresolved.

43–6. Nor does the new dawn resolve the *pena* of the gypsies as a whole. In the final lines the parallel between the search of the roosters and the search of the gypsies as represented by Soledad Montoya is finally broken: the cocks have found their dawn; Soledad and the gypsies have not. The delight of the dawn urges upon us, by contrast, the persistence (with *hidden course* and *far-off dawn*) of the gypsies' own black sorrow.

8. SAN MIGUEL (GRANADA)

'Esto es una romería,' commented Lorca when he sent a draft of the poem to Guillén (III, 894). In fact it is a very specific *romería*, the *romería de San Miguel*, celebrated annually on 29 September and formerly one of the most important events of the year in Granada, especially in the popular Albaicín quarter of the city. From an early hour people converged on the area around the Church of San Miguel el Alto, overlooking the Albaicín, to enjoy themselves, to attend mass and to pay homage to their archangel, the captain of the heavenly hosts. By the 1920s, however, reports suggest a falling-off in enthusiasm: 'el cerro no estuvo lo animado que en aquellos felices pasados años (para los antiguos), que no volverán' (*El Defensor de Granada*, 30 September 1922). Lorca's poem captures this nostalgia of the 1920s, as well as his own view of Granada as turned in upon itself, devoid of a sense of adventure.

4. Sunflowers were especially associated with Saint Michael's Day. A pointer, then, to the vendors with their wares; but also, metaphorically, to the illusion of the coming day.

7-8. *The brackish dawn creaks* (*crackles, rustles*) *in the twists and turns* (*in the angles*) *of the air*.

9-12. The real-life mules had eyes veiled in night (5-6). Now, as the dawn appears, cosmic mules of heaven close their own *quicksilver* eyes (i.e. the stars fade), with a tender farewell to the hushed half-light.

15-16. *mad and uncovered* (*naked*), in tacit contrast to the tamed water of Granada's irrigation channels, '[que] no es un agua loca que va donde quiere' (III, 320).

17-28. Lorca here evokes Bernardo de Mora's statue in the Church of San Miguel el Alto. Behind the altar a glass screen (*vidrios*) separates the nave from the 'camarín' (*la alcoba de su torre*) where the statue of Saint Michael stands surrounded by four lights (*faroles*). The boyish figure of the saint, with echoes of an oriental thousand and one nights (*efebo de tres mil noches*), sumptuously attired in female dress (*lleno de encajes . . . / enseña sus bellos muslos*) and with a fine plume of feathers on his head (*plumas*), is treading, somewhat delicately, on the prostrate figure of a demonic, tailed Satan, his right arm upraised with three arrows in his hand (*el gesto de las doce*), threatening the demon beneath his feet. But despite this threat there is no trace of violence in the saint's face, 'pues sólo se observan en los serenos ojos y en las demás hermosas facciones, la calma, el reposo de los justos, el reflejo del Empíreo' (*DG*, 29 September 1908; cf. *cólera dulce de plumas y ruiseñores*). In place of the warrior archangel of Christian tradition Lorca finds, in Mora's statue, a pointer to Granada's oriental past.

29-32. These lines take up the dawning vitality of the new day (cf. 13-16) and develop the contrast to the intervening description of Saint Michael, with a joyful opening of balconies and the appearance of more and more people.

33-6. Girls from the popular quarter are chewing the traditional sunflower seeds, with a notable demythicising of the *girasoles* of line 4 and a characteristic Lorcan pointer to lost illusion that is reinforced by the description in lines 35-6. There are similar indications in the rest of the section, culminating in the *bishop of Manila* (also, effeminately, *with Manila shawl*, traditionally worn by women on that day), *blind with saffron and poor* (very different from the warrior bishops of Christian tradition), a reflection of Saint Michael's own effete orientalism and withdrawal from life (*lejano de las flores*, the one; *ciego de azafrán*, the other). Even the *two-edge mass* seems to echo the sexual ambiguity of the saint.

47–8. *with his petticoats laden with sequins and lace* (strictly *insertions* [of lace or embroidery]).

49–50. In early Renaissance painting Saint Michael is commonly depicted with an orb or scales of justice in one hand and a sword in the other. In the context of Lorca's poem *rey de los globos* is clearly ironic (with a suggestion of glass bowls — of the *faroles* — and balloons) and the effect is increased by *números nones* (*odd numbers* but also with echoes of *andar de nones*, *to have nothing to do*). Saint Michael is magical and insubstantial.

51. primor: ms (III, 895), *Litoral* 1 (1926), 1928, 1929, 1935, Ag, MH; primer: 1937, 1938, MGP. *Primor* is confirmed by the recently published complete version of Lorca's lecture, 'Cómo canta una ciudad de noviembre a noviembre': 'Primor berberisco de gritos y miradores es la Granada vista desde el Cerro del Aceituno [where Saint Michael's Church is situated]' (III, 331).

9. SAN RAFAEL (CORDOBA)

This is one of the most difficult poems in the book, with a deliberate creation of *misterio confuso* (14) in Part I and gradual clarification in Part II. As a starting-point it is helpful to know something about Saint Raphael, the guardian archangel of Cordoba, and about the history of the city.

The only occasion on which the angel Raphael is named in the Bible is in the Book of Tobit (5–12), where he appears as a guide and counsellor to the young Tobias. While Tobias was washing his feet in the River Tigris a huge fish leapt from the water and tried to devour him. At Raphael's bidding the young man caught the fish, killed it and later used its heart and liver to cast out devils from his bride and its gall to cure his father's blindness. Because of this, Raphael is revered for his powers of healing and is identified with the unnamed angel of healing who 'went down at a certain season into the pool and troubled the water' (John 5:4). Saint Raphael's image abounds in Cordoba, most characteristically as a statue on top of a column, known locally as a *triunfo*. There are references in Lorca's poem both to the biblical story and to Cordoba's present-day cult of the saint.

Cordoba's history is impressive: under the Romans it was the capital of Further Spain (Hispania Ulterior) and later of Baetica (approximately Andalusia), becoming one of the most Romanised cities in the Peninsula, with a notable school of writers and orators whose influence extended to Rome itself; then, under Moslem rule (711–1236) and especially during its period as capital of the Caliphate of Cordoba (926–1031), the city was the centre of Moslem power and culture in the Western world, as well as being the greatest intellectual centre in Europe. Cordọba, then, stands out as 'romana y mora' (Antonio Machado) and both civilisations have left the imprint of their passing. The duality underlies Lorca's poem and explains many of its difficulties.

4. Possibly an actual Roman statue; more probably Cordoba itself.

5–8. The reflection in the water (*cristal maduro*) is seen as a superposition of successive layers — flowers, carriages, clouds — pressed between glass.

9–10. The children may be weaving baskets, as several critics suggest. Like Boyer I prefer a metaphorical interpretation (i.e. they weave their song). Cf. 'Cuando ve llegar a la muerte, el ángel vuela en círculos lentos y teje con lágrimas de hielo y narcisos la elegía que hemos visto temblar en las manos de Keats' (III, 314).

13–18. After the *misterio confuso* of the opening lines Lorca offers the first clear polarisation of elements: on the one hand the uncontoured architecture of shade and smoke; on the other, the austere splendour of marble base. But there have been earlier — vaguer — pointers to the same duality, starting with the opening lines (*orillas de juncos* vs *romano torso desnudo*). It is worth considering them.

19–22. Filigree delicacy of the breeze, joined with the solidity of triumphal arches. An even clearer pointer to the two great ages of Cordoban history, with *triunfo* also as an echo of Saint Raphael who will eventually be shown to reconcile Rome and Islam.

23–6. The Roman element is clear, with the water resounding under the arches of the famous Roman bridge. The tobacco sellers are presumably associated with smuggling and thence with North Africa (the Moslem heritage again). The *roto muro* suggests also a *granadino*'s playful response to Góngora, a native of Cordoba, who exalted Cordoba's 'excelso muro' and contrasted it with the 'ruinas y despojos' of Granada. There are other notable echoes of Góngora in this poem. Lorca, we know, lectured on Góngora's poetry in 1926 (III, 223–47) and was much involved in the 1927 tercentenary commemoration of Góngora's death.

27. A reminder of Tobias's fish, of course, which joins the two Cordobas (now clearly contrasted).

35–8. The meaning, hitherto misunderstood, follows naturally from the Roman/Moslem duality — and from the story of Tobias. The surface of the water is still undisturbed, but the young boys, like the biblical angel of healing, are about to 'trouble the water'. Tauntingly they ask the fish whether he prefers the broken surface in Roman terms (as a bacchanalian reflection of the flowers along the river bank) or in Moorish terms (as a leaping reflection of the Moslem *media luna*; 'Islamismo, mahometismo', DRAE).

43. *aljamiado.* Usually refers to a text written in Spanish but with Arabic characters. Saint Raphael, then, is both Christian and Moslem. Cf. 'San Rafael, arcángel peregrino que vive en la Biblia y en el Korán, quizá más amigo de musulmanes que de cristianos, que pesca en el río de Córdoba' (III, 344).

10. SAN GABRIEL (SEVILLA)

Lorca completes his triptych of archangel poems with an annunciation *romance* in which Saint Gabriel appears to a gypsy girl, Anunciación de los Reyes, and announces the forthcoming birth of a child to her. But Saint Gabriel is not, as had been said, the patron saint of Seville. Nor is he especially associated with Seville. It is Anunciación who justifies the connection, for the patron saint of the archdiocese of Seville is Nuestra Señora de los Reyes. The patron saint, then, is presented as a 'highly favoured' gypsy girl, 'blessed among women' (Luke 1:28). I reject suggestions that the poem is blasphemous (Cobb), demonic (Umbral) or burlesque (Harris). It is the most delightful poem in the book, with all the delicacy and charm of a Fra Angelico Annunciation and with similar stylisation and a similar integration of the biblical Annunciation into a contemporary, local context.

1–6. Note the stylising, five-line build-up, finally resolved in *ronda la desierta calle*, which echoes the best known of *sevillanas* ('Ronda mi calle') and thus associates Saint Gabriel especially with Seville (cf. *biznieto de la Giralda*, 33).

21. *tamer of turtle-doves* (Campbell) or *white moths* (Gili) or possibly *milk-white steeds* ('caballo de color muy blanco', DRAE). Andalusian responses suggest *doves*. This also accords best with Lorca's extensive use of Christian iconography: here, the dove that commonly appears in paintings of the Annunciation to indicate the descent of the

Holy Spirit. Saint Gabriel, who brings glad tidings, is naturally an enemy of willows, the traditional tree of lamentation (22).

25–6. The gypsies have clothed his statue in the church and deserve to be rewarded by the annunciation of a gypsy Christ.

27. The name effectively brings together biblical event, typical gypsy surname (Reyes) and local patron saint (Nuestra Señora de los Reyes). The echoing of a well-known *petenera* (a type of Andalusian *cante*) in 27–30 suggests that Anunciación is an archetypal 'linda gitana'.

28. *richly mooned* (cf. 'blessed art thou among women', Luke 1:28) *and poorly dressed.*

32–3. Again the bringing together of Christian annunciation (with the traditional white lily, present in almost all early paintings of the event) and local reference (*biznieto de la Giralda*, the famous cathedral tower).

37–8. *campanillas.* Both *bell-flowers* (in harmony with the stylising imagery) and *little bells* (in celebration of the glad tidings).

40. *with three nails of joy.* But the three nails recall the traditional three nails of the Crucifixion. Even in joy misfortune threatens (cf. 54, 65).

41–2. *Your radiance opens jasmine flowers on my flushed face.* Stylised suggestion of pallor.

69–70. The stars that became bell-flowers and bells, in joy at Saint Gabriel's mission (38), finally turn to everlasting flowers, eternalised by the Annunciation. But in an Andalusian context — and in the context of Lorca's poetry — it is difficult to escape also the death association of the *siempreviva* ('Siempreviva de la muerte, / flor las manos cruzadas', II, 936). As with the repeated three wounds, even amidst joy tragedy threatens.

11. PRENDIMIENTO DE ANTOÑITO EL CAMBORIO EN EL CAMINO DE SEVILLA

Antoñito, said Lorca, is a 'gitano verdadero, incapaz del mal' (III, 345). He is also, together with Saint Gabriel, Lorca's most attractively presented male protagonist. In this poem we see him, noble, hand-some and carefree, on the road to Seville to see the bullfight. But he is arrested by civil guards, rebuked by the narrator for his cowardice in submitting to arrest and finally locked up in prison.

5–8. Olive complexion and lunar magic (5), easy-going elegance (6), glossy black locks over his forehead (7–8), with a suggestion also of peacock ostentation (*pavón, pavonada*).

19. *larga*. A particularly elegant bullfighting pass, much associated with the gypsy school. In 17–20 nature takes up Antoñito's *anda despacio y garboso* (6), with similar *garbo* in its echoing of the bullfight that Antoñito should have been present at, and, in 21–4, apprehensively awaits — and even encourages by example — the possibility of escape. But Antoñito submits meekly to his arrest (25–8), with significant parallels and contrasts to the resonantly epic opening lines.

37. The *old blades* (the gypsies of old) are quivering with anger at Antoñito's betrayal of his gypsy lineage.

42. A scornful suggestion (especially in this primitive world where wine and brandy suggest macho blood and vitality) that, whereas Antoñito merely took the lemons out of delight in visual alchemy (to see the water turn to gold), the civil guards, more practical and mean-minded, stuffed them into their knapsacks.

12. MUERTE DE ANTOÑITO EL CAMBORIO

The alleged coward of the previous poem, meekly submitting to arrest, here appears in all his macho grandeur in a fight to the death. Moreover, his opponents are now not mere civil guards but gypsy cousins worthy of the fight. Narrative and causal relationships are characteristically muted. It is not certain that the fight is a consequence of the action in the previous poem but the juxtaposition of the two poems and several cross-references suggest that it is. Antoñito has betrayed his gypsy lineage and *voces antiguas* (3), echoing the earlier irate *viejos cuchillos* (11:37), herald retribution. For Lorca, it seems, gypsy mores, with their exaltation of machismo and family honour, are another element of gypsy — and human — repression.

5–8. *Bites of wild boar* and *soaped dolphin leaps* as pointers to animal vitality (cf. *hard-maned*, 20, which suggests also the proud gypsy profile).

13–16. Further bullfighting imagery (cf. 11:17–20): *rejón, lance* (for bullfighting from horseback); *verónica*, a specific bullfighting pass with the cape.

26. *Benamejí*. A village in the province of Cordoba, not far from Cabra and Montilla.

27–8. 'For he knew that for envy they had delivered him' (Matthew 27:18). I offer this as one of approximately a dozen echoes in this poem and the previous one of Christ's crucifixion and/or the associated *pasos* (tableaux) of Holy Week. Much of Lorca's characterisation, including that of Antoñito as a would-be man of peace, depends on such echoes (Introduction).

29–32. Note Antoñito's narcissistic delight in his dandified appearance, with a further bullfighting echo in *corinto* (*maroon, wine-coloured*), one of the classic colours of the bullfighter's *traje de luces*.

41. *Three spurts of blood.* Hardly a fortuitous echo of the *tres balas de almendra verde* in the Annunciation poem (10:65). Narrative and anecdote are of course wholly changed but biblical resonances abound in these poems. Antoñito is presented as a gypsy man of peace ('gitano verdadero, incapaz del mal'). But in a world of violence one cannot always submit meekly.

43. *living coin:* true currency, but also the proud profile again (cf. 1:25–7, 14:54–7).

45–8. The traditional laying-out, appropriately with angels in attendance.

13. MUERTO DE AMOR

One of the most hauntingly mysterious poems in *Romancero gitano*. Recall Lorca's comment on 'Romance sonámbulo': 'hay una gran sensación de anécdota, un agudo ambiente dramático y nadie sabe lo que pasa ni aun yo, porque el misterio poético es también misterio para el poeta que lo comunica, pero que muchas veces lo ignora' (III, 341). The doubt starts in the opening section where the boy is traditionally seen as the *muerto de amor*. For a number of reasons that I have developed elsewhere — for example, the title of the poem, which suggests an already present death (as do the *cuatro faroles*, 6, suggestive of a wake) and the protective, down-to-earth response of the mother (3–4, 7–8) — I prefer to see him merely as a witness, intrigued, as children are, by the presence of death and by the wake that is taking place in the almost mythically exalted *altos corredores* (2). For the rest I am inclined to find, as in the previous three poems, continuing biblical and iconographic resonances that give religious significance to the title and universality to the poem. Notable throughout is the repeated, almost obsessive echoing of the scene of death suggested in the opening lines.

1–2. Rizzo and Velasco quote three traditional songs with an identical first line, all with religious connotations. I quote one of the three:

> ¿Qué es aquello que reluce
> en aquel monte florido?
> Es Jesús de Nazareno,
> que con la cruz se ha caído.

9–12. An ominous moon — dissociated by *ajo* from Romantic tradition; with waning (*menguante*) suggestive of death (*agónica*) — evokes correspondingly ominous resonances in the draping of yellow hair over yellow towers.

17–18. After the superb personification of night, with dogs in pursuit at the mystery of the unknown (13–16), *un olor de vino y ámbar* points again to the wake in progress.

21–6. There is a suggestion of shattered cosmic harmony in the broken arch of midnight, while oxen and roses sleep, innocently unaware of the tragedy around. For possible further resonances, see Introduction, pp. 57–8. The clamorous *cuatro luces* point yet again to the wake.

27–34. The funeral procession: women (the ultimate sufferers for Lorca) escort and weep over the dead body, at rest in death but bitter at the cutting short of youth and vitality.

39–42. Anecdotally we return to the child of the opening lines. But the resonances, now, are wider. Aided by the exclamatory sense of *madre* it is as though, beyond the child's involvement, the narrator, overcome by the tragedy, intervenes also on his own behalf.

43–6. Mirrors are shattered by the agony of bloodshed, with insistent repetition of the magical number seven, heavy with religious resonances of cosmic significance (cf. 'And out of the throne proceeded lightnings and thunderings and voices: and there were seven lamps of fire burning before the throne, which are the seven Spirits of God', Revelation 4:5).

14. ROMANCE DEL EMPLAZADO

An *emplazado* is a man summoned to appear within a certain time before a judge, in this case God. The poem opens with the torment of the protagonist, unable to sleep, his eyes fixed on the harsh but so far unidentified destiny that awaits him (1–13). The world around serves to emphasise fate's relentless power (14–21). The torment is explained in the central section: on 25 June El Amargo was warned to prepare for death, for he would die within two months (22–41). Saint James approves the decree and the heavens turn their back on the condemned man (42–5). The decree is finally fulfilled and El Amargo accepts his fate with stoic dignity (46–57). The emphasis on heralded misfortune and fatal outcome helps to make this one of Lorca's most characteristic poems. But the theme is also traditional and the much-narrated story of Ferdinand IV 'El Emplazado' seems especially relevant, with the king's allegedly unjust execution of the Carvajal brothers, the younger brother's appeal to God to summon the king before Him within a period of thirty days and the fulfilment of this appeal: 'Antes de los treinta días / malo está el rey don Fernando, / el cuerpo cara oriente / y la candela en la mano. / Así falleció su Alteza, / de esta manera citado' (*RVC* 64, n. 10). Characteristically Lorca's *emplazado* has been democratised: on the plane of anecdote he is a mere gypsy; on a universal plane he is Everyman.

6–13. His eyes are unable to give themselves up to the tranquil voyage of sleep but, ever watchful, fix on the destiny foretold for him: harsh (*norte, metales, peñascos*) and unalterable (*norte, naipes helados*). Note especially how Lorca uses words less for their immediate dictionary meaning than for their emotive resonances.

14–17. A shallow stream tends to flow with much froth and broken surface; a deep stream with smoother surface but greater power. As Lorca explained in his lecture on Góngora, *buey de agua* is used in Andalusia to indicate the latter (III, 224). The poet here accepts the traditional image but characteristically revitalises it and brings out its primitive force by interpreting it literally and showing the oxen attacking the boys who bathe in its *cuernos ondulados* (with further literalisation, since *ondulados* refers to the effect of the water's *ondas*). In context, then, the *bueyes del agua* appear as an image of unstoppable fate. So do the hammers in the immediately following lines (with echoes of the *cante* known as *martinete*, in which hammers provide the only accompaniment to the singer).

22–41. Note Lorca's use of hard imagery: specific physical indications with emotive significance: cut the oleanders (a traditional flower of death; cf. 'dolor de cal y adelfa', I, 161, 'lo amargo de la adelfa', I, 353), paint a cross on the door with your name beneath, hemlock and nettles will spring from your side . . . and an echo of the earlier — and similar — *norte* / *de metales y peñascos* (with *aires fríos* now to confirm the coldness implicit in *norte*).

42–3. Saint James's Day is 25 July, appropriately at the mid-point between 25 June and 25 August. The Milky Way is popularly known in Spain as the *vía de Santiago* and is suggested by the saint's nebular sword. Lines 44–5 exploit these cosmic resonances with an image of abandonment that gives fuller significance to *soledad* in the opening *¡Mi soledad sin descanso!*

50–7. Emphasis on the Roman — statuesque — dignity of El Amargo's passing, with further hard imagery. In death too one is alone, but finally at rest: *soledad con descanso*.

15. ROMANCE DE LA GUARDIA CIVIL ESPAÑOLA

Lorca's gypsy world is a world under threat: the death-bringing moon (Poem 1), the pursuing wind (Poem 2), black angels (Poem 3) . . . . The main part of *Romancero gitano* concludes with a mini epic in which the gypsy world is finally destroyed, by the gypsies' traditional real-life enemies, the Civil Guard.

9. *blotches of ink and wax.* A pointer to the Civil Guard's involvement with official reports and religious processions. One finds a similar mingling of dread and scorn throughout the opening section, with physical features that characteristically take on wider resonances: black that suggests something beyond mere colour, lead that points to lack of humanity, patent leather that is extended from the traditional hat of the Civil Guard to the soul, dark hunched figures that in context suggest deformity. But physical observation too is notable: for example, the *miedos de fina arena*, like grains of fine dry sand that yield to one's tread.

17–24. The contrasted festive world of the gypsy, childlike and magical, with an echo of festive gypsy songs in *En las esquiras banderas* and suggestions of a fairy-tale world of pumpkins and gingerbread houses. But after the dark opening section, the repeated *¡Oh ciudad de los gitanos!* of longing and illusion seems singularly forlorn, especially at its second appearance, accompanied by 22 which associates it, nostalgically, with the past.

28. Like mythical Vulcans, forging illusioned *soles y flechas*, amidst a magical *noche que noche nochera* that suggests children's rhymes and 'el ritmo de bulerías y villancicos gitanos' (*1*, 281).

41–8. An evocation of a children's Nativity crèche or tableau.

60. *la benemérita.* The official title of the Civil Guard.

67. *Siemprevivas* are traditionally associated with death (cf. above, note to 10:69–70).

69–70. *They advance in double file. A double nocturne of cloth.* Cf. *Jorobados y nocturnos* (9) and *capas siniestras* (90).

85–8. The lines echo a well-known traditional *romance* on the siege of Alora:

> Viérades moros y moras
> todos huir al castillo:
> las moras llevan ropa,
> los moros harina y trigo
> y las moras de quince años
> llevaban el oro fino,
> y los moricos pequeños
> llevaban la pasa y el higo (*RVC* 79).

88. monedas: ms (*A* I, 198), Ag, MH; moneda: 1928–1938, MGP.

93. *En el Portal de Belén.* A traditional line in *villancicos*, with continuing stylisation of the scene, as also in the involvement of Saint Joseph and the Virgin (with a suggestion of gypsy cure elevated to cosmic status).

107–8. A reminder of numerous fifteenth-century paintings of martyrdoms of saints, most clearly the martyrdom of Saint Agatha.

113–16. After the devastation, the personified appearance of the dawn as it becomes visible on the skyline.

124. *Interplay of moon and sand.* A final reminder of the poet's illusioned vision of the gypsy world.

16. MARTIRIO DE SANTA OLALLA

Romancero gitano concludes with three 'romances históricos' that stand somewhat apart from the rest of the book. The first, originally referred to by Lorca as 'Romance del martirio de la gitana Santa Olalla de Mérida' (III, 901), evokes the martyrdom of the young Eulalia, probably in AD 304, more than eleven hundred years before the first gypsies entered Spain. Lorca's source was almost certainly the 215-line Latin hymn to Saint Eulalia by the Hispano-Roman poet Prudentius (348–410). But much has been changed and in the present context Lorca's *romance* can best be considered independently. Beyond the progression indicated by the subheadings critics have noted a colour gradation from night to the cold light of dawn and on to the iridescent light of Paradise. There is conceivably an even more important progression: from the ruin and mutilation of Roman Merida, destined to collapse entirely at the coming of a new dawn, through Olalla's martyrdom, which even amidst horror suggests that new dawn, and on to a contrasting evocation of the dead Olalla and of a world reborn. I find also echoes of the Crucifixion that serve to elevate Olalla's martyrdom and to broaden its significance.

1–2. The Lorcan horse of ill omen (cf. 15:29–30).

3. An earlier manuscript version, 'mientras juegan a los dados', points more clearly to paintings of the Crucifixion in which soldiers are depicted playing dice for Christ's clothes (cf. Matthew 27:35). *Dormitan* may echo the slumbering insensitivity of the disciples during Christ's agony in the garden (Matthew 26:36–46).

5–6. *Minervas.* Variously interpreted as olive trees (the tree of Minerva) and shrubs (regional usage). Possibly mutilated statues, with a contrast to Daphne, whose arms sprouted leaves. In any case, an image of lifelessness.

7. *suspended water*, which I take to be frozen, perhaps as snow, along the crests of the rocks; another image of lifelessness.

9–12. Images of inertness and mutilation, elevated from *torsos yacentes* (soldiers and statues) to cosmos; imminent total collapse associated with the awaited dawn.

14. The cockcrows of course, with a possible echoing of the Passion (Matthew 26:74–5).

16. *Cantaores* are reputed to shatter wineglasses with their singing.

17–18. The sharpening of instruments of torture (*knives and sharp-curved hooks*).

19. Image of power and agony.

20–2. The coming dawn, with a mingling of delight (*nardos*) and suffering (*zarzamora*). An echo perhaps of the biblical crown of thorns (torment and new life).

23–4. The approach of spring. But the goddess of flowers and spring is so far naked and the water, it seems, is still frozen.

25–6. Recalls paintings of other martyrdoms in which breasts are cut off and placed on a tray (cf. 15:107–8).

27–42. Especially notable is the vitality released by the martydom: spurting veins, sex that trembles like a bird ensnared, lopped-off hands that leap, milk that flows, trickles of blood that oppose the searing flame.

43–6. The centurions, it seems, have been stirred from their lethargy and clamour at the gates of heaven, possibly in challenge, more probably in remorse and homage (cf. Prudentius's executioner who 'amazed and confounded broke away and fled from what his hands had done', 173–4; cf. also the biblical Passion: 'Now when the centurion saw what was done, he glorified God', Luke 23:47).

51–62. A symphony in black and white, with a surrealist image of tailors' dummies, black like the charred body, that weep their mutilated silence over the snow-covered countryside.

65–6. A possible echo of the biblical lance in the side (John 19:34).

67–74. Apotheosis, with a monstrance that shines amidst a world reborn, with stream gorges where there was frozen water, nightingales in branches where there were *brazos sin hojas* and leaping colours where there was inert whiteness. Olalla's elevation is finally confirmed by association with Catholic liturgy and direct quotation from it.

17. BURLA DE DON PEDRO A CABALLO
(ROMANCE CON LAGUNAS)

All pre-*RG* versions of the poem (two in manuscript and one printed) bear the sole title 'Romance con lagunas'. The earlier manuscript is dated '28 de diciembre 1921'; the later one, sent for pre-*RG* publication in *Mediodía* of Seville (1927), is dated '28 de diciembre 1921–1927' (*4*, 165). The implication is that Lorca saw 28 December ('Día de Inocentes', the nearest Spanish equivalent to April Fool's Day) as important, and in 1928 he incorporated his jest or leg-pull into the definitive title. There is also a possible echo, within the poem, of Don Bueso, the comic protagonist of numerous popular *romances* (*1*, 291). But critics are in notable disagreement about the identity of Lorca's Don Pedro, and the knight of Olmedo, the Apostle Saint Peter and Peter the Cruel have all been proposed, with extensive study and profuse evidence. It is not certain that the question merits so much emphasis. Lorca intentionally withheld specific identification, suggesting resonances rather than establishing equations (cf. *¿Es Belén?*, 28). In what follows I concentrate on the poem itself and survey critical debate elsewhere. What seems clear, amidst simplicity of language and difficulties of resonance, is that the poem presents a characteristic Lorcan quest for illusion that results, characteristically, in failure and death. The form of the poem, allegedly a *romance* but with a notable variety of line-lengths (from 3 to 11 syllables) and with departure, at moments, even from alternate-line assonance, suggests that the jest is directed, in part at least, at the reader as well as the protagonist. In anticipation of the protracted identification debate, perhaps also at critics.

1–12. In the context of *Romancero gitano* the combination of journey, lamentation, unbridled horse (cf. 7:16–18) and quest suggests already the inevitable failure. Marcilly has emphasised line 8 as a pointer to Saint Peter's quest for the bread and kiss of Christ and he may well be right. But one must be wary of transposing Lorca's mystery into Marcilly's desired 'clarté'. The mystery is intentional and is intensified by the personified involvement of wind and windows.

13–23. Apparent simplicity of language again conceals difficulties of resonance. A *laguna* is a lake and one can emphasise the magical, childlike vision of the moon bathing in the lake and rousing the envy of the distant moon that it reflects, with a child appropriately telling the moon to clash the cymbals (the two moons). But a *laguna* is also a lacuna or gap in a manuscript. It thus points to a loss of narrative as words disappear. But the loss of narrative is seen by *romance* enthusiasts as a positive merit, a means of liberating the reader's imagination, and Lorca, here as elsewhere, plays down narrative in his own *romance*. The bathing moon can be seen as a magical releasing of imagination that rivals the magic of the moon on high and should appropriately join with it.

24–37. The narrative returns. Various identifications have been proposed for the distant city of gold — Medina Sidonia, Seville, Jerusalem —, but Lorca leaves the mystery unresolved (*¿Es Belén?*). What is important — and clear — is that the object of Don Pedro's quest is a realm of illusion (distant, golden, amidst a wood, enveloped in perfumes, bathed in light), with echoes of countless legends, romances and fairy tales. And the journey is typically arduous and forbidding, with pointers to ruin and ill omen. We are poised, then, characteristically in a Lorcan context, between illusion and disillusion. Poplars and nightingale take up and confirm the duality. 26. ciudad de oro: ms (MGP, 180), Ag, MGP; ciudad lejana: *Mediodía* 7 (1927), 1928–1938, MH. Joaquín Romero Murube has accepted responsibility for the traditional error. As editor-in-chief of *Mediodía* he wished to keep Lorca's manuscript for himself, copied it out for the printer and apparently, like many a medieval scribe, jumped back two lines and wrote *lejana* (24) again instead of *de oro* in line 26. Lorca presumably used a cutting from *Mediodía* for the 1928 edition, failed to notice the change and the error was perpetuated in successive editions of the book (see *Insula* 94, October 1953, 5).

38–45. Again the narrative is submerged, this time under a rippled surface, with a circle of birds and flames that suggests, like the earlier moon, the released imagination. But, as I show elsewhere, there is also a corresponding musical image, with ripples as the strings of a guitar, the circle of birds and flames as the sound-hole and the lake itself as the body of the instrument. Surrounding it, I suggest, are the *aficionados* of *cante*, well aware of the unexpressed causes of sorrow.

46–63. The failed quest, with death and pathos — a procession to the cemetery, Don Pedro's dead horse, a sorrowful bleating, a mythical fairy-tale creature that has shattered its only horn, the burning city, weeping — and a reminder of the basic duality of illusion (the star to the north) and questing traveller (the sailor to the south).

64–9. The words are finally submerged, fused with the sediment of successive generations of similar stories. Don Pedro as an individual is forgotten, a mere playmate of frogs. In these lines, it seems, Lorca offers the key to his avoidance of specific identification and anecdote. It is not the individual narrative that matters, but the wider, universal resonances. Not what distinguishes, but what joins. Don Pedro is Don Bueso and the Knight of Olmedo and Saint Peter and Peter the Cruel. But above all, perhaps, he is Everyman in his vain quest for illusion. The theme of the poem is thus identical to that of others in *Romancero gitano*, including two of the most notable, 'Romance sonámbulo' and 'Romance de la pena negra'.

18. THAMAR Y AMNON

The Old Testament story of Amnon's rape of his half-sister Tamar (II Samuel 13:1–22) has many traditional *romance* versions and was dramatised and novelised by leading writers of the Spanish Golden Age. In his lecture-reading Lorca emphasised the *romance* tradition and, together with the Bible, it was doubtless this that influenced him most. In certain ways, he declared, the poem is more shocking than 'La casada infiel' but it is protected from a similarly sniggering response by its greater difficulty. This combination of popular tradition and poetic difficulty is striking and merits thought. 'Thamar y Amnón' is arguably the most densely written poem in the book, with resonances that extend far beyond the biblical rape.

4. The thunder and lightning of an approaching storm, with rumblings of animal and cosmic vitality that promise fertility (*siembra*), in contrast to the detached — and infertile — turning of the distant moon over barren lands.

6. A harp image, used elsewhere by Lorca ('El arpa y su lamento / prendido en nervios de metal dorado', I, 959), and this will later be important. But in the immediate context it suggests tension, with pointers to steely sinews, between heaven and earth, as though bracing the universe in harmony.

9–12. Drought and searing heat, of course, but with wounds that suggest also the imposed vitality of *tigre y llama*, especially since the earth *offers itself*, as though in sexual surrender.

13–14. An earlier *cantando* (ms) has been muted to *soñando* to suggest rather than state explicitly Thamar's vision of innocent love, in contrast to the scarred earth.

15–16. Echoes of the cold, detached moon, and a further contrast to the burning earth.

17–18. Enticing nakedness but also coldness (*agudo norte*) that both contrasts with the earlier *agudos cauterios* and suggests their possible threat.

19–20. Usually interpreted as a quest for coolness for her burning body (e.g. 'Begs snowflakes for her belly hot / And hail for her bare arms', 56). I interpret differently: Thamar is associated with the cold detachment of the moon and looks to her own body for defence against the threatening heat (and against the threatening sexuality of *tigre y llama*): i.e. *begs snowflakes of her belly / and hailstone of her shoulders.*

24. Further coldness, with a possible echo of paintings of the Immaculate Conception where cherubs encircle the feet of the Virgin Mary. But purity is here associated also with life-condemning frigidity. Loughran has perceptively associated Thamar with Selene, the moon-goddess.

25–8. In contrast to Thamar, enticing but frigid as she lies on the roof-top (cf. the moon's cold seductiveness in Poem 1), Amnón, spying on her from a tower, burns and quivers with sexual desire.

29–32. Critics disagree about whether these lines refer to Thamar or to Amnón. In context it seems clear that they refer to Thamar (especially since an earlier draft depicted Amnón *asomado a la ventana*). Thamar is pierced by Amnón's gaze, with echoes both of Cupid's arrow and of the earlier *rumores de tigre. Clavada* too is obviously relevant to *tigre* and *heridas.*

33–6. More clearly still Thamar is here associated with the moon of lines 1–2 — and with the moon of Poem 1 —, now significantly closer to the earth.

37–8. 'So Amnon lay down, and made himself sick: and when the king was come to see him, Amnon said unto the king, I pray thee, let

Tamar my sister come, and make me a couple of cakes in my sight, that I may eat at her hand' (II Samuel 13:6).

39–40. Eyes that take flight, with an echo of the earlier *alero* that prompted their flight, and the transference of suffering from Amnón to the room where he lies.

41–4. The barren earth again, with just a sign of vitality, akin to the earlier *heridas cicatrizadas*.

45–8. The suppressed vitality of water and a pointer to the biblical serpent, here associated with Thamar, similarly singing (21–2) and *tendida* (29–30).

49–56. Amnón's burning desire and Thamar's coldness. But why is Thamar *troubled with distant traces* (or freely, perhaps, *sullied by things long past*)? Eve's temptation of Adam is a possible explanation, for Thamar is presented as another temptress. But there are several echoes in this poem of the rape of Bathsheba by King David, the father of Tamar and Amnon (II Samuel 11:2–4). In either case, a typical Lorcan pointer to the weight of heredity.

57–60. Another contrast between Thamar's frigidity and Amnón's passion.

56–8. Inaccessibility (*pechos altos*) and enticement (*dos peces que me llaman*), with a suggestion of vitality confined (cf. 45–6).

69–76. The world around characteristically responds to the violence, with neighing horses and a conflict between contained heat (cf. 67–8) and the plunging roots of the vine (cf. 25). The *corales tibios* recall earlier pointers to vitality in the sterile earth (10, 43–4).

83–4. *Pistons and thighs* suggest the sexual act, while clouds stop short in horror at the rape.

85–8. An echo of a gypsy bridal chorus to proclaim the bride's virginity:

> En un verde prado
> tendí mi pañuelo;
> salieron tres rosas
> como tres luceros.

91–2. The coming of the new day brings with it echoes of the earlier sexual imagery of vine and fish (compare the duel of the lilies with the air in 6:46–7).

93–100. In the Bible story of Amnon's rape of Tamar there is neither flight nor the shooting of arrows. But there is in the immediately adjoining episodes and Lorca has characteristically fused them.

Thus, in David's scheme for ridding himself of Bathsheba's husband, 'the shooters shot from off the walls upon thy servants' (II Samuel 11:24), and after Tamar's brother Absalom killed Amnon in revenge for the rape, 'every man gat him upon his mule, and fled' (II Samuel 13:29). One recalls also God's wrath at David's own rape: 'Thus saith the Lord, Behold, I will raise up evil against thee out of thine own house' (II Samuel 12:11). David's final cutting of the strings of his harp appears in context as a typically Lorcan recognition of the inexorable power of fate. The harp that sounded in harmony at the beginning of the poem will sound no more.

Printed in the United Kingdom
by Lightning Source UK Ltd.
129556UK00001B/22-24/P

9 780719 078255